T0128968

COMO SER UN BUEN LÍDER

PRINCIPIOS DE LIDERAZGO QUE
CAMBIARÁN TU VIDA PARA SIEMPRE

SOLO TU PUEDES MARCAR LA DIFERENCIA

NACISTE PARA SER UN BUEN LÍDER

COMO SER UN BUEN LÍDER

DR. GUIDO RAFAEL VACA

Número de Control de la Biblioteca del Congreso de EE. UU.:   2012915096
ISBN: Tapa Blanda   978-1-4633-3759-9
                   Libro Electrónico   978-1-4633-3758-2

Información de la imprenta disponible en la última página.

Fecha de revisión: 05/07/2016

Para realizar pedidos de este libro, contacte con:
Palibrio
1663 Liberty Drive
Suite 200
Bloomington, IN 47403
Gratis desde EE. UU. al 877.407.5847
Gratis desde México al 01.800.288.2243
Gratis desde España al 900.866.949
Desde otro país al +1.812.671.9757
Fax: 01.812.355.1576
ventas@palibrio.com
424974

PRINCIPIOS DE LIDERAZGO QUE CAMBIARÁN TU VIDA PARA SIEMPRE

DEDICATORIA

Con todo mi Corazón, dedico este libro a mi lindo Padre que ahora goza en las mansiones celestiales, en presencia de los ángeles y mi Dios, y a mi linda Madre que está conmigo siempre dándome sus sabios consejos día a día, los que me formaron desde temprana edad, pusieron en mi mente y Corazón un sí, a lo que otros me decían que no, que me inculcaron el verdadero amor por la vida y por mi Dios, me enseñaron a perseverar, en saber planificar antes de lanzarme al mundo de lo desconocido, y que gracias a ellos, hoy soy lo que soy, con alegría en mi Corazón les digo a mis lindos padres que los sigo amando más y más.

AGRADECIMIENTOS

Gracias mi Dios, por ser el dueño de mi ser y llegar cuando más te necesite, a ti sea la Gloria y la honra cada minuto de mi vida que me das, por darme este gran privilegio de escribir estas palabras que van desde los más profundo de mi mente y corazón, un trabajo personal que está basado en experiencias vividas, atravesó de los años que me has permitido, como humano, cristiano y profesional realizar, debo mi principal agradecimiento a mis hijos, mi familia que de una u otra manera han sido, son y seguirán siendo el principal motivo de inspiración, para salir adelante, hasta encontrar la cima del éxito y la paz de la montaña, donde se reflejan todas las metas y anhelados sueños hecho realidad, para que ahora pueda gozar de esa verdadera felicidad y compartir con Ud. De que nada es imposible en la vida para el que quiere triunfar.

UN AGRADECIMIENTO ESPECIAL

Hago público mi agradecimiento especial, a mis pastores: Reynaldo y Noemí Mejía, de la Iglesia, LOS UNO EN CRISTO; localizada en la ciudad de Paterson NJ, por llegar a mi vida en los momentos más difíciles, cuando por unos instantes me sentí muy solo y abandonado, donde pensé que todo estaba perdido, pero que gracias a Dios, llegaron en el momento preciso y a la hora indicada, para extenderme su incondicional ayuda cuando más la necesitaba, que Dios derrame sobre sus vidas lluvia de bendiciones.

Í N D I C E

PRÓLOGO 21

EL POR QUÉ DE ESTE LIBRO 29

INTRODUCCIÓN 35

¿QUÉ ES UN LÍDER? 41

FACTORES QUE DETERMINAN UN BUEN LÍDER............................79

CARACTERISTICAS DE UN BUEN LÍDER 111

COMO SER UN BUEN LÍDER......................................141

REGLA DE ORO... 156

lucha por tus grandes sueños, con el compromiso que salga de lo más profundo de tu alma, mente y corazón, con esa fe que DIOS, te.........

Indicará a seguir por los mejores caminos, que te conduzcan hacia la meta final, haciendo trabajar esa luz interna que brilla dentro de ti sin.........

Dudar de para aquel que se esfuerza y persevera, todo lo imposible lo hace posible, con alegría en tu corazón, venciendo cualquier obstáculo que puedas..........

Encontrar en el devenir de tu vida, desarrollando a cada instante, buenas palabras, sonrisas de aliento y pensamientos constructivos, que edifiquen tu vida, para que puedas ser....

Recordado por todos los seres que más amas y por el mundo entero por ese legado de superación.

Bienaventurado el hombre que halla la Sabiduría y que obtiene la inteligencia Ya que es el árbol de la vida a los que de Ella echa mano. Prov.: 3 (13-18).

Con este profundo pensamiento espiritual que ha marcado mi vida en toda su dimensión, dejo ante Ud. mi amigo lector, mis palabras plasmadas en mi inspiración textual, de que su vida de éxito y fructífera prosperidad, depende mucho de esta gran enseñanza espiritual, que nuestro señor Jesucristo nos dejó como gran legado sobre la SABIDURIA Y INTELIGENCIA, que tú y yo debemos día a día cultivar y los efectos a corto plazo, que puede producir son sorprendentes, si de verdad estás de acuerdo con mi forma de pensar, una gran verdad que la quiero enfocar como testimonio y pueda que tu vida llegue a mejorar como lo pudo hacer con muchos hermanos en Cristo, lo hizo conmigo, y también lo hará contigo; si de veras tu anhelo es triunfar, para dar ese gran paso en tu vida de cómo ser un buen líder, para que puesto en práctica estos principios, podrás guiar, controlar, encaminar, motivar, animar, capacitar a los tuyos, a la cima del éxito total, de tal manera que debemos reconocer que la sabiduría que gira en torno a tu vida, edifique no solo lo interno, sino también lo externo, para que algún día lo puedas reconocer y que mejor también lo puedas compartir con el más necesitado, para que también, sean los grandes beneficiados de una completa felicidad, aduciendo de que con fe, amor y perseverancia el esfuerzo por llegar al destino final, se vuelve manso como una paloma, de tal manera que es importante reconocer que le debemos dar mucha prioridad al momento presente que es lo que cuenta en nuestras vidas, lo que la mente usa esa gran línea divisoria de un pasado y un futuro para ubicarte en la realidad del presente lo que tienes para triunfar, desarrollando tus proyectos por los cuales debes luchar.

PRÓLOGO

El ser humano en la vida no tiene por qué sentirse inferior, ni tampoco ser inferior a nadie, de hecho todos nacimos iguales privilegiados para triunfar en la vida, no para fracasar, esos pensamientos de fracaso no están en los planes de Dios, cuando tuvo la brillante idea de crearnos a su imagen y semejanza, con esos grandes atributos que tú y yo los tenemos, así que con el siguiente comentario que quiero llegar a tu vida, te puedas dar cuenta, de que es el mejor día, y una excelente oportunidad para que despiertes, y te pongas a trabajar por esos grandes anhelos que hay en tu mente, cuerpo y corazón.

En el año 1994, comienza mi anhelada aventura, de hacer realidad mi gran visión, que un día se impregno en mi vida, dándome una intranquilidad emocional, que a decir como verdad, era imposible conseguirlo, ya que los criterios negativos de quienes me rodeaban, eran de desmayar ante mi existente realidad, la verdad que se apoderaron de mi todos estos pensamientos de renunciar ante mi visión, la razones eran muchas para claudicar, sin dinero, con muchas deudas, distanciamiento de mi familia, el idioma, cultura, costumbres, la no capacidad para ejercer trabajos rudimentarios, racismo, características de personalidad que también fueron muy difícil para hacer realidad mi gran visión, pero aquí es donde quiero dar como testimonio, de que quien tiene y acepta a Dios, como el único que puede solucionar tus grandes necesidades, y suplirte de esa fuerza genuina, para que en esta ocasión pueda decir y compartir con sinceridad que me siento muy feliz, de haberlo podido lograr.

Comienzo con mis grandes sueños, al llegar al país de las grandes oportunidades, una gran y dura verdad que se reflejaba en mi diario vivir, ya en territorio americano comienzan los grandes azotes de desesperación, pero para aquel que sabe confiar en Dios, lo imposible se vuelve posible, de tal manera que con las duras pruebas que se agigantan día a día, es donde se ve y se prueba a los grandes hombres de fe, para que así puedas llegar a donde nadie antes lo pudo hacer, así que, mi gran odisea sacude las fibras más sensibles de mi ser, alejándome en su totalidad de mi gran visión.

Mi primer obstáculo de crecimiento comienza a golpear mi dura y difícil realidad, el idioma Ingles no me permite llegar a donde mi mente deseaba estar, no obstante se presenta las mejores opciones de superar este inconveniente y es así que, comienzo a recibir mis clases de Inglés en un Instituto de Idiomas, respaldado por el gobierno de turno en ese entonces Bill Clinton, comandaba la nación, llego a terminar mis estudios en el idioma Ingles en el año 1998, como segunda enseñanza, obteniendo mi diploma, apto para trabajar en el mercado anglosajón, donde mi capacidad en el conocimiento del idioma Ingles, me permitía ser una persona bilingüe, dándome un gran impulso hacia mis metas, sirviéndome como gran base de una sólida e intangible motivación, para seguir en busca de lo que un día soñé.

En el año 2006 pude obtener en la escuela FOX SCHOOL REAL ESTATE, de la ciudad de Paterson New Jersey, el certificado para poder trabajar COMO AGENTE DE BIENES RAICES, dándome la gran oportunidad de hacer experiencia en la compra y venta de bienes raíces, en el estado de new jersey, desarrollando una buena capacidad para obtener un contacto local, nacional y porque no decirlo mundial; tuve la gran experiencia de conocer diversidad de culturas, que me motivaban cada vez más a seguir en esta Hermosa profesión, donde pude adquirir, la suficiente confianza en mí mismo, de que lo que estaba haciendo y desarrollando era de mi completo agrado.

Así mismo la gran experiencia de conocer el mundo financiero, estrategias que dichas instituciones desarrollaban, para dar y complacer, a la infinidad de clientes, en la compra y venta de diversidad de casas, linda experiencia, que me fue impactando para que pueda seguir trabajando arduamente, en el cumplimiento de mis anheladas metas.

A comienzos del 2007, comienzo mis estudios universitarios que es donde siempre fue mi deseo el sentirme, útil para lo que estaba en mi proyecto, desarrollándose en mi ese deseo ferviente de seguir perseverando, no obstante los grandes impedimentos que se me presentaban eran de un total rechazo, pero como siempre vuelvo y lo repito quien tiene a DIOS, en su Corazón lo tiene todo, y él siempre fue el que me dio la inteligencia y la paciencia para que pueda confiar, y con amor y fe en mi Corazón pude entender, que siempre estuvo, esta y seguirá a mi lado, hasta que me otorgue el ticket que me llevara a su morada, es menester enfocar en este gran paso de mi vida, que mi familia fue y sigue siendo también el principal centro de motivación, han entendido mi largo caminar, aunque muchas veces también me decían, que es muy sacrificado, ya que como emigrantes que somos, la principal actividad de responsabilidad, es el trabajo, y por esta razón pensaban que no me daba tiempo para realizar lo uno y lo otro, a medida que el tiempo, me iba dando la satisfactoria razón en lo que había emprendido, comencé a sentir ese apoyo incondicional a mis grandes sueños, y es así que gracias a las bendiciones de mi Dios, corono en mis estudios a finales del año 2009, en la Universidad Atlántica Internacional de la ciudad de MIAMI-USA, obteniendo una MAESTRIA, en negocios internacionales, para la cual me había preparado(budines management), dándome el gran privilegio de poder trabajar como empleado de algunas financieras en el estado de NEW JERSEY, NEW YOPRK Y PENSILVANIA (BFS), que en español quiere decir asesor de servicios financieros; sirviendo a la comunidad en el Adelanto de préstamos de dinero, por sus negocios que en Ingles se dice CASH ADVANCE.

Mis sueños no terminan ahí, sigo perseverando por lo que tanto había anhelado, al llegar a este país, de manera que se me da la oportunidad en el mes de noviembre del año 2009, matricularme para seguir mis estudios y poder conseguir el objetivo deseado, de obtener el título que me llevara al EXITO, de ser un profesional en el país de las grandes oportunidades, como lo es Estados Unidos de Norteamérica, y es así que en el año 2012, pude hacer realidad mi gran anhelado sueño de convertirme en un hombre de éxito, que con capacidad, dedicación y perseverancia lo pude conseguir, a esto se suma todo el gran apoyo espiritual, familiar y de algunas amistades que siempre confiaron en mi persona, y estuvieron conmigo en la dura batalla de la vida, en las buenas y en las malas, que me dieron ese apoyo incondicional, gracias de todo corazón, y pude graduarme como, DOCTOR EN BUSINESS ADMINISTRATION, en Atlantic International University de la ciudad de MIAMI USA, dando gracias, honor y honra a mi Dios, por tan merecido logro.

Es menester dar a conocer el significativo apoyo y ayuda de mi madre, mis hijos, hermanos y toda mi familia que son el centro de mi inspiración, que a diario me motivan a seguir viviendo por ellos, y para ellos, para poderles entregar un respaldo que los haga feliz, mis lindos hijos, también forman parte fundamental en mi vida, Christian, Viviana e Ismael Vaca, para que día a día siga luchando y perseverando, por tener una vida mejor.

Exhorto para que comiencen a trabajar por sus anhelados sueños, que de la misma manera como, Dios lo está haciendo con los grandes de espíritu altivo, de llevarlos a la cima del éxito, también lo está haciendo conmigo de llevarme hacia la victoria con un solo propósito de reconocer que en Dios lo tenemos todo y con completa seguridad lo hará contigo, si te decides a dar el primer paso, para llegar a donde tu visión te lo indicare, de manera que solamente tu serás responsable de lo que puedas alcanzar en esta vida, te exhorto para que comiences hoy mismo, solamente tu marcaras la diferencia en el mañana.

EL POR QUÉ DE ESTE LIBRO

La verdad es de que sentí el deseo grande de plasmar con mis ideas, este libro que está enfocado a todas las personas que tienen ese hambre de liderar, para que de alguna, manera pueda en algo aportar con este trabajo, que lo he desarrollado con todo el deseo de que tu también puedas utilizar ese gran talento, esos grandes dones que Dios deposito en ti, quiero motivarte, para que puedas trabajar con todo el entusiasmo que hay en tu corazón, especialmente a ti joven, hombre o mujer, que estas en la mejor etapa de sus vidas, para que puedan convertirte en los lideres que lo anhelan, no obstante los impedimentos serán nuestro peor enemigo en esta sociedad, pero que si de veras hay en tu corazón ese gran deseo como lo tengo yo, seguro que somos y seremos los privilegiados de sonreír en el mañana y si me lo permites, que pueda decir más allá de lo que te imaginas, el mundo, la sociedad, tu comunidad te lo agradecerán y también podrás impartir, tus grandes aportes y conocimientos de liderazgo al que de veras lo desee en un futuro no muy lejano.

Recuerdo cuando en una ocasión, tuve el gran privilegio de escuchar de labios de un grupo de adolescentes, el gran deseo que se reflejaba en sus rostros el sentirse importante frente a la sociedad, hasta tal punto que miraba el contingente de interés por parte de ellos, en capacitarse, me contaban historias donde la vida les daba una linda oportunidad, para que lo puedan desarrollar hoy y con planes a un corto plazo, los deseados líderes, que el mundo los necesita, así que esta y más historias que llegaron a mis oídos para poder trabajar por mi libro, y en aquel entonces despertó en mi ser, el deseo grande de poder escribir temas que estén relacionados en la rama de liderazgo, una linda oportunidad para llegar a Ud. con humildad y sencillez, con estos aportes, que de seguro vas a meditar, pensar y actuar, para que haya una razón muy motivadora en mi persona de que valió, mucho todo el esfuerzo empleado en realizar mi sueño, este libro dedicado para Ud. de 'COMO SER BUEN LIDER', en esta sociedad.

Aquel mes de octubre, comienzos de un otoño, con vientos que atemorizaban el amanecer y atardecer de una embriagante tranquilidad de vida, con sonidos que desde los cuatro puntos cardinales se escuchaban muy seguido, anunciando el fenecer de un árbol ahí dormido, donde sus hojas en un vivir de Gloria, figuraban las siluetas más hermosas, se convertiría en un capítulo más de importancia para mi vida, no solo me daba la pauta para profundizarme en mis aventuras, sino que la culminación de hacer realidad uno de mis más anhelados sueños, el escribir este libro para Ud. Se despertó el deseo más ferviente de plasmar con mis ideas, pensamientos, luego vinieron palabras expresando la vivencia mía de un mundo interior, y estas a su vez fueron convirtiendo en frases, para que vengan párrafos, y finalmente mi anhelado libro que de seguro ayudara a edificar tu vida.

Gran parte de lo que escribo es el resultado de ese gran legado de mi padre, el profesor, supervisor y Doctor Héctor Vaca, que ahora goza en ese terreno celestial en compañía de mi Dios y los ángeles, supo inculcar en mi desde temprana edad, las sabias enseñanzas y consejos sanos de edificación, que ahora se refleja en mí, un hombre de bien, caracterizado por saber escuchar, aprender y perseverar en los caminos de la vida que de por si son duros, pero que gracias a ese gran potencial que Dios nos da, nos permite que podamos aplicar, para que sea el engranaje que lubrique los obstáculos más grandes que tengamos que recorrer, hasta encontrar el buen sabor de la vida, donde fluye leche y miel, para los que confían y tienen fe de hacer lo imposible en cosas posibles y puedas ver que las ventanas de los cielos se abrirán en lluvia de bendiciones para ti y para mí.

La importancia que tiene este libro para ti como una fuente de consulta a tus interrogantes, donde puedas reforzar tus grandes anhelos, deseos, aspiraciones que tengas para con tu vida, de salir adelante, tal vez en oportunidades pasadas nunca lo habrías hecho mejor, pensaste que todo estaba perdido que ya no habían esperanzas para ti, o que se yo, o tal vez todos tus anhelos de triunfar ya fenecieron, te exhorto para que te levantes de donde ahí tu estas, y des ese gran paso de fe, lo puedes lograr si de veras te propones, adelante que nunca es tarde para emprender, en lo que en tu mente lo puedas visualizar, déjame compartir estos principios que te los hago llegar para ti con todo mi corazón, esperando que de una u otra manera te puedan servir, para que alcances hacer realidad lo que antes no lo habías podido conseguir.

Presta mucha atención al momento
Que pasa, a lo que estás haciendo
Ahora; porque del ahora depende tu
Mañana.

Con nuestros pensamientos y palabras,

Construimos el mundo en que tú y yo

Vivimos.

INTRODUCCIÓN

El verdadero significado de liderazgo, lo heredamos de nuestro señor Jesucristo, cuando atravesó de su gran sabiduría, supo liderar, al mundo entero, generando una estabilidad, confianza, amor y seguridad en todos quienes somos sus seguidores y lo podemos particularizar, cuando formo su grupo de los 12 apóstoles, donde les inculco como trabajar, en grupo, desarrollando y fortaleciéndolos en ellos las habilidades y grandes dones y talentos innatos, para que puedan cumplir con sus grandes objetivos, que fue el de cristalizar sus metas grupales, como lo enfoca el concepto de liderazgo, que es donde se trabaja, por dirección de alguien con una buena capacidad, profundo conocimiento, se habla también de un poder sano y una buena imagen que les de seguridad a sus seguidores, trabajando voluntariamente y entusiastamente en el cumplimiento de sus metas grupales.

La palabra liderazgo está en la mente y en los labios de toda persona, especialmente en la gente joven, hoy en día dicen que quieren ser líderes, especialmente la juventud que promueven un liderazgo con conocimientos no fundamentados que no tienen el enfoque vital de como liderar una sólida organización, no reúnen los adecuados principios de un correcto liderazgo, que están siendo manipulados por falsos líderes que no tienen ni la más mínima idea de COMO SER UN BUEN LIDER, en esta sociedad, de cómo es lo que trabaja este tópico en el ser humano, Los líderes de hoy se basan en paradigmas caóticos de retraso social, como lo podemos observar; en las grandes gangas, que los grandes propósitos de estas organizaciones no se ajustan a las necesidades de una sociedad en desarrollo, de tal manera que si estos líderes lo aplicaran con temas de engrandecimiento moral, ético y espiritual, las cosas serían muy diferentes, como este tópico lo amerita. O se enfocaran con objetivos que apunten a un buen desarrollo social, donde se puedan mezclar conocimientos científicos, intelectuales y espirituales, podríamos decir que están contribuyendo al progreso de una fructífera sociedad y consecuentemente serian estas personas bautizados como los grandes líderes que la patria, la comunidad y el mundo los necesita.

Hoy en día todos nacemos con principios de liderazgo, a medida que vamos desarrollando nuestra vida, se puede ver si cultivaste esas cualidades y características de ser un líder, donde la familia, la sociedad y la comunidad sean las beneficiadas, o lo contrario a todo esto sucedería, o el enfoque incorrecto de ser un líder, donde puedas que toda esa gama de riqueza espiritual, esté en el olvido, o ese gran potencial se esfumara, como se pierden las nubes en el firmamento, dejando a su paso mucho malestar, sufrimiento y tanto dolor, pero estoy aquí para decirte, que es el momento, es el hoy, para empezar tu meta que antes no la habías planificado, desempaca lo que tienes en el baúl de los sueños, destapa esa ceguera espiritual, donde tienes tus ojos espirituales cubiertos por una gruesa capa de desánimo, de fracaso, de desesperación, de falta de fe, de no creer en ti, de entregarte más, a descubrir tu vida espiritual y puedas emprender con fuerza, con esa luz y esperanza que ya Dios deposito en ti, y puedas ser un hombre o una mujer de abundante prosperidad.

El liderazgo es la fuerza de la vida, la gran fuerza de la imaginación, que te permite tener visión, para que puedas apreciar y observar no solamente de donde estas liderando hoy, sino que donde podrás llegar el día de mañana.

Prov.: 37 (34).- espera en Jehová y guarda Su camino; Y él te exaltara para heredar la Tierra.

CAPITULO UNO
¿QUÉ ES UN LÍDER?

La interrogante que planteo es una pauta que me permite enfocarme muy a fondo, sobre mi libro, de cómo ser un buen líder, la verdad es de que esta pregunta la sigo haciendo y compartiendo con mucha frecuencia por donde me dan la oportunidad de compartir estos grandes principios, que por cierto es la base primordial para edificar tu vida de felicidad. El gran objetivo de mi pregunta es inculcar en tu mente y en la de los demás seres esta gran verdad, para que juntos podamos organizar, crear, trabajar, disfrutar, reír, hablar, si es que hay que llorar, también juntos lo podamos hacer, por darles un mañana mejor a los que de ti dependen para poder vivir.

El ser LIDER, implica en muchos factores como personal, moral, social, político, económico, psicológico, intelectual, religioso, etc. Para poderlo desarrollar ya que nos hemos visto en la gran necesidad de poder reforzar nuestros grandes anhelos de liderazgo, con personas con grandes experiencias, en lo personal lo puedo testimoniar, de que la Biblia ha sido y seguirá siendo la fuente de consulta más inspiradora para desarrollar mis grandes objetivos, se suma también a mi investigación o este tópico, personas con gran capacidad de liderar como Martin Luther King, la Madre Teresa de Calcuta, Jongeward Dorothy, Dra. Scott, William Arntz, Betsy Chasse, Mark Vicente, Abrahán Lincoln, Dalie Carnegie, Benjamín Franklin, Sir Isaac Newton, Galileo Galilei, Giordano Bruno, William Tiller, Joe Dispensa, Cristóbal Colon, Adolfo Hitler, nuestro señor JESUCRISTO, Nicolás

Un líder recibe a sus seguidores con paz, amor y alegría, en su Corazón, aunque muchas veces estos grandes detalles alegres y espontáneos, conquistan un Corazón y consuelan un dolor.

Copérnico, Francis Bacon, y muchísimos más que se podría mencionar de cómo pudieron liderar. Con sus grandes legados; que marcaron la historia de la humanidad para siempre se desarrolló en mí el gran concepto de lo que es ser un líder.

Líder es aquel, que tiene la capacidad para poder influenciar en tu vida, y poder desarrollar el gran talento que Dios, deposito en ti, con entusiasmo, con tu propia voluntad en desarrollar tu trabajo, y así obtener tus objetivos previstos.

En el ámbito espiritual; es aquel que trabaja por hacer trabajar esos grandes dones que Dios deposito en ti, por el bienestar de su grupo, dándoles con su gran ejemplo, el gran motivo y razón para que puedan seguir sus sabias enseñanzas, en el merecido cumplimiento de sus metas grupales.

Los líderes de esta sociedad, la nación y el mundo entero, necesitan este gran contingente para despertar confianza y seguridad en sus seguidores, y convertirse en el ejemplo viviente que se necesita para desarrollar y formar un mundo de paz, una vida con principios que te permitan ser feliz, y poder formar las deseadas organizaciones que tanto se anhela, donde se pueda ver, el gran adelanto, el progreso, desarrollo, seguridad y el avance total, en toda su dimensión.

El aspecto espiritual que es lo más importante que se pueda argumentar en la vida de un líder, principal argumento que se debe enfocar para que todo objetivo alcanzado tenga su aprobación total, deben estos líderes presentar una gran capacidad, para inspirar a todos sus seguidores a desarrollar el rol de saber liderar, no obstante cabe mencionar que algunos expertos, en este gran tópico lo consideran, al liderazgo como un arte de influenciar en otras personas para alcanzar sus anheladas metas.

Lo explico más detalladamente, cuando el liderar se convierte en un ARTE, con este minucioso ejemplo; el director de una orquesta sinfónica, es considerado un líder, porque se esfuerza para que todos los integrantes cumplan con sus objetivos, comienza por entrenar para que cada, persona desarrolle sonidos agradables a nuestros oídos y corazón, para que ya ordenadamente se conviertan estos sonidos en agradables canciones, y satisfechos de haber cumplido sus objetivos grupales, concluyendo así la definición como un arte para liderar.

A esto se suma la gran importancia que el líder debe, ser responsable a su gran función de liderar, porque si no existe esta adecuada función específica de cómo trabajar, por alcanzar los objetivos deseados, consecuentemente vendría la gran calamidad del fracaso y lo que afectaría en su totalidad al progreso de nuestra comunidad y sociedad y de todas las organizaciones existentes.

Siempre los líderes, están atentos para escuchar críticas honestas, que recibir muchas veces elogios que están vacíos por sus seguidores.

La importancia de reconocer quien eres y
Y por donde vas, don estas hoy y donde
Llegaras mañana; con fe y perseverancia
Alcanzaras, que tu luz interna que brilla
En tu corazón, resplandezca los caminos
Obscuros que te han impedido llegar al
Éxito total.

El líder siempre limpia sus caminos

Que le impide desarrollar su gran

Visión, con actitud positiva y gran

Compromiso de hacer que todos

Sus sueños sean una realidad.

LO QUE ES UN LIDER

Es la persona que siempre va delante y muestra el camino a sus seguidores. No es dominante ni controlador en lo absoluto de su vida, pero siempre incentiva y apoya para motivar a todos los que se encuentran en su alrededor, como por ejemplo podemos mencionar, la responsabilidad que tiene un padre frente a sus hijos, que los motiva segundo a segundo en sus diferentes actividades. Él puede organizar, dirigir, juzgar y tomar las mejores decisiones sabias que le van a dar mucha satisfacción a todos y esto atraerá el mejor ambiente de seguridad a toda su familia.

Un buen líder debe tener la habilidad de saber gobernar dentro y fuera del círculo que se encuentre, como lo podemos observar aquel padre de familia, como se organiza cada vez mejor con su familia en su círculo de paternidad.

La verdadera responsabilidad de un buen líder se encuentra en el don de dar servicio a su grupo, atendiendo sabiamente cualquier inquietud o situación que a sus seguidores les pueda ocurrir. La meta de un verdadero líder debe enfocarse en los términos que le produzca un crecimiento total como:

Adiestrar a su gente

Desarrollar seguridad

Liberar sin tratar de impedir ni controlar a sus seguidores.

El propósito de un líder, también se enfoca en descubrir quién es cada uno de sus seguidores, el don particular que ejerce cada individuo frente a una determinada organización, hasta llegar a conseguir su gran madurez sin distorsionar el gran propósito que tiene Dios para con sus vidas.

EL LIDER ANIMA

El líder como animador les da a todos y aquellos que están bajo su responsabilidad, su gran corazón de padre, su completa seguridad y la absoluta confianza de poder realizar más de lo que ellos se puedan imaginar, para que estén listos en desarrollar por su propia cuenta, lo que antes estaba planificado.

Es aquel que les da ánimo y es muy paciente, en especial cuando se trata de su gente que le sigue, siempre los está animando de diferentes maneras y en diferentes posiciones, con su elocuente palabra, profetizando palabras de superación, con mucho gozo, mucha alegría

Los líderes miran en todos sus seguidores, un gran futuro que los lleva hacia la felicidad.

como el líder lo pueda expresar, de tal manera que debemos seguir estos buenos y fructíferos principios de crecimiento, a cada momento, sin criticar, ni herir sus sentimientos, ni tampoco juzgarlos cuando las cosas no les sale como lo tenían planeado. El intento de seguir perseverando en sus diferentes áreas de liderazgo, los hará más fuertes y más seguros en la gran batalla, y que necesitan desarrollar poco a poco esa fe, que los hará grandes para que puedan conseguir hacer realidad sus grandes metas, lo que en otras ocasiones no lo pudieron lograr.

EL LIDER LLEVA LA CARGA

Siempre acepta con amor y alegría ser responsable de su grupo a como dé lugar, de tal manera es muy fiel y se puede imitar y aprender cosas positivas de él, nunca se da por vencido ante cualquier situación, porque no lo considera como una opción en su vida, debido a que su corazón y su mente se encuentra dotado de esas actitudes mentales positivas, que lo hacen único en su organización, aunque cualquiera de los que integran su grupo le pueda fallar, él siempre se mantiene en pie de lucha, consecuentemente no puede fallar.

Grandes testimonio llegaron a mi mente, de aquellos líderes que me supieron contar, de cómo ha sido, es y seguirá siendo la lucha de un líder, comentarios que llegaron a mis oídos, de ver como sus seguidores fallaron cuantas veces, recibieron de sus seguidores la traición, fueron muchas veces usados, pero ellos siempre se mantuvieron fieles, perdonaron sus fallas, como nuestro señor Jesucristo, nos perdona por nuestros pecados, porque nos ama de corazón, ese es el mismo rol y función de un líder que debemos imitar, el saber perdonar de todo corazón.

EL LIDER ES UN ESTABILIZADOR

Siempre se mantiene estable en su posición, depende mucho de su organización, es muy seguro frente a ellos, está dispuesto a romper la misma roca por enseñarles cómo hay que perseverar, para que puedan entender que con paciencia y amor se puede llegar a donde nadie lo pudo antes hacer.

Toda buena dadiva y todo don perfecto desciende de lo alto, de nuestro Padre Celestial

Santiago 1:17

Tenemos que imitar a nuestro Dios y a los grandes líderes con conocimientos, con principios y valores bíblicos, muy firmes, con convicciones que nos permitan conocer la verdad, la que nos conducirá al éxito, tenemos que creer en nosotros, ser muy íntegros como estos líderes que se esfuerzan día a día, por entregarnos las mejores alternativas y maravillosas opciones que nos lleven a descubrir la verdadera paz.

EL LIDER ES PROVEEDOR

Siempre el líder provee o suple las diferentes necesidades de aquellos que lo ameriten, prepara la provisión para cualquier necesidad, con mucha anticipación, en otras palabras es muy precavido, de lo que sin planificar se pueda presentar, todos sus seguidores que están bajo su dirección, nunca están desamparados y necesitados por algo que el líder no lo pudo cumplir, tienen los recursos necesarios para obtener más confianza y crecimiento.

Con el siguiente verso bíblico podemos entender mejor este tópico, nos aclara mejor su mensaje, nos da el correcto discernimiento, para que miremos que el secreto para poder desarrollar un verdadero liderazgo, está en que nos enfoquemos más a menudo, en la sagrada Biblia, la que nos guiara por los mejores senderos de nuestras vidas.

Para que los líderes puedan recibir su gran motivación, acuden a la oración espiritual donde encuentran el mejor momento para demostrar su fuerza de impulso hacia la meta.

Porque si alguno no provee para los suyos, y mayormente para los de su casa, ha negado la fe, y es peor que un incrédulo.

1 Timoteo 5:8

Un líder que provee, es una fuente de todo lo sentimental, emocional, espiritual y material, para todos aquellos que dependen de él, como es un buen proveedor también se convierte en un buen dador, destacándose por ser generoso haciendo el bien a todos los hombres que encuentre a su paso, y a la humanidad si es posible, es muy ahorrativo, se enfoca muy bien en saber controlar las finanzas, pensando siempre en el gran legado que pueda dejar a sus seguidores.

EL LIDER ES UN BUEN TRASMISOR

Un líder trasmisor, es aquel del cual absorbimos todo, como cuando la esponja seca, la introduces en el agua, absorbe todo lo que pueda en su paso, así mismo es el hombre que se considera un buen líder, deja que todos sus discípulos aprendan todo lo que sea necesario de su líder, que lo caracteriza como un buen trasmisor en sus conocimientos espiritual, intelectual, social, ético, moral, político y religioso. Su mentalidad nutrida de sabiduría, conocimiento, su carácter moldeado a imagen y semejanza de nuestro señor Jesucristo, sean los ingredientes necesarios, para inculcar en los demás.

EL LIDER ES UN ADIESTRADOR

Es aquel del cual sus seguidores y todos los que en el creen, obtengan las mejores experiencias, destrezas, habilidades, para poder enfrentarse en sus grandes adversidades, como lo relata la maravillosa historia del rey David, cuando lo pudo vencer al gigante solamente con una diminuta piedra, para coronarse como gran REY, pero que habilidad y destreza de este barón de Dios, que hoy lo tenemos en nuestro corazón, como gran legado de superación.

Cuando el líder hace conocer este gran detalle de adiestrador, es porque el ya obtuvo la victoria antes, con sabiduría e inteligencia, conquistar el mundo desconocido y en un futuro no muy lejano, todos sus seguidores podrán marcar la diferencia.

EL LIDER NUTRE

Es aquel que alimenta el carácter y potencial dado por Dios a los hombres y mujeres de hoy, hasta llevarlos a una completa madurez de sus vidas. Él es el que cuida a sus seguidores, como cuida un pastor a sus ovejas, con mucha sabiduría, enseñanzas e inteligencia, para mantenerlos muy seguros de sí mismos y que puedan confiar, los nutre de ese gran amor, los trata con mucho cuidado, así como lo hace un padre a su hijo, como Dios nos cuida a nosotros, de esa misma manera el líder lo hace con su grupo, hasta llevarlos a una mejor dimensión de éxito.

EL LIDER LEVANTA TU AUTOESTIMA

Cuando el líder los ama a sus seguidores, es porque cree en ellos, se sabe relacionar, usando la mejor comunicación de poder tener un buen dialogo con su gente, les entrega su completa confianza, como lo cumple un padre de familia de verdad con sus hijos, les hace conocer lo valiosos que son, y que son únicos en esta sociedad, no son copia son originarios levantándoles el ego a cada instante, estos líderes no dan mente a ninguna situación negativa, no presten oídos a palabras que no edifiquen, ellos siempre estas descubriendo ese potencial que hay dentro de ellos, desarrollando destrezas que los mantengan alimentando su espíritu, con actividades de crecimiento personal y también en grupo, profetizándoles a cada momento lo grande que son y seguirán siendo en esta vida, bendiciéndolos

Los pensamientos que los líderes utilizan para llegar al éxito, salen del alma acompañados de sabiduría e inteligencia que solo Dios les puede otorgar.

dándoles ese amor ágape muy incondicional, para que se sientan muy apreciados y valorados, que piensen que algo hermoso hay para ellos, si se esfuerzan de corazón, y consecuentemente el éxito será la eterna compañía.

EL LIDER ES UN MAESTRO

Siempre está dispuesto a enseñarles los mejores caminos a seguir a sus fieles seguidores, está listo para inculcar la verdad a donde tienen que llegar, como llegar y cuando llegar, el que enseña la palabra de Dios, el que lo puede todo, el que nunca falla, el que bendice, sana, liberta y el que te provee de abundante sabiduría, el líder también está listo para enseñarte los mejores principios, los buenos valores que los ayuden y que los guíen en sus vidas, y sobre todo los valores morales para que vivan en rectitud.

EL LIDER ES UN BUEN INSPIRADOR

Un buen líder es aquel, que anima y también inspira a su gente para que lo sigan en sus determinadas áreas, sin lugar a duda que estos principios llevados a la vida práctica, tienen efectos sorprendentes; de manera que me enfoco más a fondo con este importante tópico, para compartir ideas, fructíferos pensamientos que con seguridad te ayudaran a descubrir el gran secreto que te ayudaran para triunfar en la vida, con el gran compromiso que tengas que hacerlo hoy mismo con tu corazón, si quieres encontrar la leche y la miel que fluye del objetivo a alcanzarlo.

En el transcurrir diario de mi vida en cuanto a mi investigación sobre el liderazgo, que no solo habla en el aspecto local sino también en un sentido general, se me da la oportunidad de poder con mis propios ojos ver, como es que las grandes potencias mundiales hoy en día son las que controlan y conquistan el mundo entero, desarrollando los mejores sistemas de vida capitalista, para dominar al mundo entero, donde los principales protagonistas de esta realidad, o de la gran película como lo quiera llamar, son los denominados y conocidos como los grandes LIDERES, que son de los cuales hoy estamos aprendiendo, para seguir adelante con sus grandes legados, de los cuales dependemos en su totalidad para nuestro propio crecimiento. Es importante dar a conocer lo que sucede en las grandes urbes del mundo, ya sea en el amanecer y en el atardecer de todos los días, los pensamientos de estos grandes líderes nunca se detienen, están en continuo proceso de trabajo, buscando y generando oportunidades de cómo salir adelante ante cualquier crisis que se pudiera presentar, incomodando el bienestar de la comunidad, como lo podemos observar con el siguiente comentario.

*L*os líderes desarrollan con mucha credibilidad la fuerza de la fe, que los llevan no donde están hoy, sino donde llegaran el día de mañana.

La gran manzana como la conocemos, el gran Manhattan, la ciudad Metrópolis, la ciudad que nunca duerme, la gran capital del mundo, bueno Ud. A lo mejor puede que haya escuchado infinidad de substanciales nombres, que la hagan única en nuestra sociedad, una hermosa y elegante ciudad donde residen los mejores líderes del mundo. Que fue para mí el principal punto de investigación en mi significativo libro de "COMO SER UN BUEN LIDER", ya que es aquí donde funcionan las grandes empresas poderosas, compañías de finanzas, como lo es el centro mundial de finanzas, WORLD TRADE CENTER, que está listo en emprender el mejor apoyo financiero, para el mundo de los negocios, no obstante que esto ha sido posible gracias a la intervención de esos grandes líderes, de los cuales quiero con Ud., compartir.

La comunidad CHINA, centro de población más popular en el mundo entero, asentados en la ciudad de Manhattan, por décadas por la calle Canal st, de la misma ciudad, la principal característica de ellos para poderlos localizar, conocido como el gran "BARRIO CHINO", para el mundo entero, la pregunta es de que porque estoy hablando de este grupo social.

La verdad es que, aquí de esta comunidad es donde pude aprender y entender de cómo es lo que trabajan los verdaderos líderes en el mundo entero, que hasta su misma vida la entregan por cristalizar sus grandes ideales, los cuales han trabajado y lo siguen haciendo,

No es todo lo que saben los lideres, lo que los hace únicos e indispensables, sino como aplican lo que saben en el desarrollo de sus grandes proyectos.

por entregarnos una solución en donde podamos gozar de nuestras necesidades, hoy nos entregan las grandes conquistas de lo que un día lo soñaron, como podemos darnos cuenta que todo lo que se mueve en el planeta tierra, con respecto a importación y exportación de cualquier producto, viene de la CHINA, cosa muy interesante y sorprendente, la respuesta a todo esto, ya está mencionada, de que hay que ser buen líder de Corazón, que hasta el momento mi asombro ha sido muy peculiar, que en ninguna otra comunidad en el mundo, lo han podido igualar, lo que ellos como, LIDERES lo hacen, de entregarse por completo a sus grandes metas, que no hay impedimento alguno que los pueda detener en hacer realidad sus grandes sueños, que hasta son capaces de entregar como lo menciono anteriormente; sus vidas mismas para convertirse en los grandes ejemplos de admiración.

Se desarrolló en mí una gran admiración por lo antes acotado, despertando ese gran deseo de poder imitar y seguir ese gran legado de esta importantísima comunidad en mi vida práctica, jamás antes en mi vida lo había podido presenciar, con otro tipo de comunidad en el mundo que habitamos, de tal manera que vale la pena detenerse a pensar muy profundamente en este tipo de liderazgo que nos ofrecen, ya que es tan primordial y muy importante para el resto de comunidades, y lo tengamos que profundizar en nuestra vida de proyectos de liderazgo personal, familiar y empresarial.

Sobre este gran tópico de liderazgo que, esta linda comunidad, lo han podido desarrollar, quiero hacer hincapié con lo siguiente para que podamos entender mejor, como es lo que un líder tiene que hacer.

EL BARRIO CHINO

Más conocido en el mundo entero por su gran masa popular de habitantes, que conforman este populoso barrio, donde los únicos habitantes que habitan, por todo el canal Street, son originarios del país de la CHINA.

Una vista panorámica del barrio chino en la ciudad de Manhattan New York.

Además de ofrecernos técnicas de cómo ser los mejores líderes en el mundo, también nos ofrecen la oportunidad de involucrarnos en sus negocios, siendo portadores de todos sus productos de fabricación, para poderlos comercializar por el mundo entero, generando una buena ganancia económica para nuestros bolsillos, por su reducido precio que lo ofrecen al momento de vender, como no se lo puede obtener por ninguna otra comunidad del mundo con esas mismas ventajas que solo ellos lo pueden dar.

Los pensamientos y palabras de un líder, hace que puedas vivir una vida de éxito.

Mi respeto muy profundo a esta linda comunidad que gracias a Dios pude conocer, su gran sencillez y humildad me ha dado la pauta para poner en práctica el principio bíblico de proverbios donde dice:

Aquel que se humilla Dios lo bendecirá

Y aquel que se ensalza Dios lo humillara

Y aquí está la conclusión mi amigo lector, de este principio, la comunidad CHINA, con sus grandes líderes hoy en día son los más alabados, reconocidos, ensalzados, por sus sencillez en el globo terráqueo, pero muy bendecidos por su inteligencia, Dios siga derramando sobre sus vidas las mejores bendiciones.

UN BUEN LIDER

Cuando emprende un buen camino, nunca se arrepiente

En ningún día de su vida, porque está muy consciente

que todos los días le dan felicidad, sacándole mucho provecho

de los días que ve mucha dificultad, obteniendo la gran

experiencia, para ser un líder sin temor, él tiene en su mente y

corazón fe, amor y mucha perseverancia, para alcanzar lo

antes prometido, siempre se mantiene, muy firme y seguro en

sus intentos que lo hacen grande, sus penas lo hacen muy

humano, las caídas lo vuelven humilde, pero siempre esta

pensando, que su liderazgo es muy seguro, de una cosa esta

muy seguro, que el EXITO, lo hace muy único, todo esto le da

siempre gracias al grande entre los grandes, al señor de señores

Al que tiene la fuerza y poder, al rey de reyes, al que desborda

en tu corazón, con abundante sabiduría, enseñanza y

inteligencia, el que te da la fuerza para ser muy valiente, el que

te da nobleza para que nadie te humille, humilde para que

nadie te lastime y ese es nuestro gran DIOS, que te impulsa y te

motiva a menudo, para que seas el gran líder que la familia, la

sociedad y el mundo lo necesita.

Siempre se puede soñar en el ser que nunca falla.

Lo que nuestra mente debe conceptuar muy elocuentemente en el diario vivir de que ser líder es muy diferente de ser jefe, no obstante mi inquietud por llegar hacia ti con mis aportes de un minucioso y exhaustivo trabajo, que mi gran deseo como aspirante de llegar a donde Dios me tiene preparado, es de inconfundible felicidad, mi intensión sana es de que puedas atesorar en tu corazón día a día el deseo ferviente de ser cada vez mejor, y prestar mucha atención a lo que pasa, a lo que estás haciendo ahora, porque del ahora, depende tu mañana, así que analiza muy detenidamente lo siguiente.

Tarde o temprano, todos descubrimos que por nuestra fuerza y conocimiento no llegaremos a ningún lado, necesitamos de la capacidad que existe más allá de nosotros mismos, un poder que solo Dios nos puede brindar.

LIDER

Tiene poder de discernimiento

Tiene una actitud mental positiva

Tiene Corazón de padre

Adiestra a otros

Bendice a todos

Trabaja en equipo

Es muy comunicativo

Está atento a escucharte siempre
No tiene obstáculos que le impidan progresar

Nunca deja nada pendiente

Sus relaciones personales son muy profesionales

Es muy culto y disciplinado

Nunca se da por vencido

Siempre está en el lugar de los demás

Su compromiso es con el Corazón

Demuestra mucha acción

La perseverancia y dedicación de un líder, hace que sus seguidores lleguen con facilidad al cumplimiento de sus objetivos.

EL JEFE ES TODO LO CONTRARIO

Siempre su humor cambia

Es muy cobarde y temeroso

Guarda siempre su posición

Condena, castiga, humilla y menosprecia

Es intolerante

Tiene complejos de superioridad

Su orgullo no lo deja actuar como es

Es muy jactancioso

Trabaja independientemente

Lo cree saber todo

Es dueño absoluto de su palabra

No acepta críticas constructivas

Deja de hacer las cosas para otro día

Es muy impaciente

Se cree dueño de sus conocimientos, desarrollándose un egoísmo fatal

Jamás te permite un crecimiento

Es muy egoísta

Se vanagloria a cada instante.

Los líderes siempre discuten con serenidad y conquistan fama de hombres sabios, inteligentes y bien educados.

En tu mente y corazón debes atesorar estos conocimientos que te permitirán, ya en la vida practica poder diferenciar, el rol que desempeña ya sea un LIDER o el mismo JEFE, es tu gran responsabilidad de elegir cuál de estas dos definiciones quieres para tu vida.

CAPITULO DOS

FACTORES QUE DETERMINAN UN BUEN LÍDER

Es importante mencionar que para que todo sea consumado se necesita de una ecuación intelectual e espiritual, cuando hablamos de lo intelecto nos referimos a que tiene que ver causa y efecto, acción y reacción, de la misma manera lo enfoco espiritualmente, obediencia más compromiso igual bendición, si mis queridos amigos; no puede existir un proyecto si no existe una base sólida y tangible de ideas y pensamientos realizables que conlleven a un propósito planteado, que se necesita para complementar este importante tópico de lo que es liderar, no solo en el aspecto social, también trabaja en tu vida familiar, personal y sus efectos son sorprendentes donde puedas ver que el éxito y la gloria de Dios está de tu lado.

Dentro de los factores que abarcan esta bendecida función de liderar, tenemos a los siguientes, que han sido muy fundamental tomar en cuenta para que todo aquel, que se proyecte con mente de liderazgo, deberá atesorar en su mente y corazón, estos principales aspectos muy importantes

PODER

No está enfocado en el dinero

CAPACIDAD PARA INSPIRAR

Buen motivador

PROFUNDO CONOCIMIENTO

Muy intelectual

UN BUEN ESTILO O IMAGEN DEL LIDER

Su presencia da mucho que decir

Su forma de hablar

Su estilo

Cuan bello es el amor de Dios que lo pudo complementar, dándonos estas bellezas para que tú y yo seamos felices.

PODER

Palabra muy profunda, que conlleva a una confusión de carácter dominante en un mundo secular, pero que en esta ocasión, es todo lo contrario de lo que tú te puedas imaginar, convencido de que nuestra mente tiene el poder de discernir todo lo que por nuestros oídos escuchamos en nuestro diario vivir, lo que nuestros ojos pueden observar y captar, y que lleguen a nuestra mente, donde nuestra memoria almacena datos, los analiza para luego proyectarlos hacia la realidad, es importante que analicemos este aspecto de la realidad, para que podamos entender el propósito grande que quiere Dios que puedas atesorar en tu mente y corazón, una gran verdad que lo he podido descubrir, atravesó de mis horas de estudio y entrega total, para conocer lo importante que es conocer la palabra de Dios, como lo dice en la biblia y nos exhorta para que nos capacitemos, sobre su palabra que es como espada de doble filo, que penetra hasta lo más profundo de tu ser, para discernir tus pensamientos y entender las intenciones de tu corazón, lo que quiero compartir es de que si la palabra poder la retienes en tu mente con una actitud mental negativa, obviamente vendrá la confusión, pero si del otro lado de la moneda esta misma palabra poder; la analizas con una actitud mental positiva entonces entenderás que lo que quiero compartir contigo podamos estar en completo cuerdo.

*N*ada es imposible para un líder proyectarse en una misión o visión que le sea imposible, cuando tiene en mente lo que quiere conseguir.

Cuando hablamos de este tipo de poder lo enfocamos en todo su aspecto, pero con mucho cuidado de no ofender la sensibilidad de sus sentimientos, con un carácter de sumisión, de humildad, de sencillez, con todos los dones del espíritu santo, se conjuga esta palabra en la mente tuya y de los demás para poder llevar a feliz término este tópico aquí planteado.

Cuando un líder reúne estas hermosas cualidades, antes mencionadas para liderar, la palabra poder trabajar, no solo en el aspecto económico, se profundiza en el rose social, que clase de personas son las que influyen y comparten tu vida, a esto se suma personas de carácter, puede ser político, social, económico, religioso, y todo lo que se puede creer que refuerza y aumenta la imagen de un líder; no bastante se puede dejar de lado su influencia para que sus seguidores puedan estar con el líder, y de tal manera que tiene que estar preparado para poder dirigir, movilizar, activar, convencer, corregir y disciplinar a todos sus seguidores, en otras palabras un poder grande para aplicar estas cualidades en toda persona que esté dispuesta a convertirse en un líder ejemplar.

El líder es vital para el progreso y desarrollo de cualquier entidad grupal, ya que dé el depende para que haya un crecimiento total.

Debemos acotar algo muy importante con respecto a este tópico que genera, el complemento perfecto para ser un buen líder, la palabra PODER, es el resultado de un secuencia de responsabilidades, donde intervienen dos factores muy importantes, como lo es:

EL DINERO
Y EL TRABAJO

El dinero y el trabajo, que sumado como una ecuación psicológica, da como resultado el poder, que todo ser humano lo anhela tener.

El dinero y el trabajo están, como es natural íntimamente relacionados, al establecer una separación entre la preocupación por el beneficio económico y todos los valores inherentes al trabajo, el dinero puede convertirse en el foco de un narcisismo laboral, dicho de otra manera, el placer que proporciona el dinero puede ocupar el lugar del placer, que proporciona el trabajo, sin embargo estamos inmersos en ese vaivén de la vida secular, que si lo tomamos por el lado más sensible de nuestra personalidad, estaremos siendo los únicos y fuertes candidatos al fracaso, en otras palabras, pérdida total de nuestra vida, donde se conjuga en tres dimensiones sobrenaturales, que lo es el espíritu, cuerpo y el alma, creados por nuestro redentor Dios.

Y que esta nuestra invitación para que podamos agarrarnos fuertemente de nuestra creencia espiritual, que para poder llegar a establecer un liderazgo, de renombre global, en nuestras vidas, busquemos las sabias enseñanzas de Dios que nos exhorta a cada minuto que entreguemos nuestro corazón para recibir sabiduría e inclinemos nuestro oído a la palabra sabía que tiene para ti y para mí.

El poder no solamente se enfoca en lo material, va acompañado de lo espiritual, emocional, familiar, físico, social y personal.

No obstante el poder es para muchos líderes como un producto muy popular, que los hace únicos en la sociedad a los líderes, se dice que las naciones luchan por él, los grandes empresarios compiten ferozmente por él, y las personas en el mundo casi en su totalidad no lo pueden tener.

En la actualidad la búsqueda de poder se acelerado a pasos agigantados, en esta época de mucha competividad, se ha invertido increíble trabajo para poder alcanzar lo, si bien es cierto las características de esta cualidad del líder tienes las siguientes funciones:

Autoridad

Prestigio

Influencia

Seguridad
Dominio

Seguridad ante todo

Respeto

Conquista

Altivo

Sin embargo debemos puntualizar, de que todas estas funciones no tienen la equivalencia total del poder de Dios, el único que puede con su palabra darle el respeto absoluto que se lo merece, la única verdad es de que el poder le pertenece al señor de señores, el que vive y reina por los siglos de los siglos en tu Corazón y en el mío.

Dios te otorga el poder que necesitas, aquel que dura para toda una eternidad, el que no es efímero, el que se compenetra en tu mente, cuerpo y corazón para toda la vida, el que debes usar para los buenos propósitos, enfocado en una vida de bendición, de progreso, de crecimiento, adelanto, unificación familiar, social y mundial, presta mucha atención en no confundir en el poder que viene del dinero, o del mercado, ese concepto aléjalo de tu mente y corazón, en su reemplazo ubica el poder de Dios, el que ejerce poder sobre todas las naciones y todos los pueblos del mundo, él es la fuente de toda la riqueza y fuerza del globo terráqueo.

REINALDO MEJIA

Un ejemplo de liderazgo espiritual, con mi pastor REINALDO MEJIA, de la iglesia los "UNO EN CRISTO", donde junto con su esposa y su digna familia, pastorean ya por muchos años, en la ciudad de Paterson NJ, donde la Gloria y la honra se la da al que vive por todos los siglos, nuestro señor Jesucristo.

Estas cualidades y características son las que reúne en su vida REINALDO MEJIA, un verdadero líder cristiano es ahora un ejemplo de LIDERAZGO, para aquellos que tengan en mente y corazón de seguir este legado, que te llevara a descubrir como la ventana de los cielos se abrirá, para derramar sobre tu vida y de los demás, lluvia de bendiciones, donde nos exhorta, este barón para que sigamos sus principios de superación.

Por sus frutos lo conocerás al verdadero LIDER, dice la palabra de Dios, y Reinaldo Mejía un ejemplo de un extraordinario líder cristiano, que con su gran capacidad intelectual y valioso profesionalismo, también se desempeña como locutor en la Radio "VISION CRISTIANA", en la ciudad de Paterson NJ, llevando la voz de Dios, al más necesitado, difundiendo con sabiduría el evangelio de salvar vidas, y también ha sido reconocido internacionalmente como Pastor, llevando su elocuente mensaje de la palabra de Dios al mundo entero, donde su único afán y interés ha sido el de que muchas vidas sean restauradas.

PROFUNDO CONOCIMIENTO

La clave máxima para ejercer con completa solidez este importante paso de liderar, nos complace hacer hincapié a las estrategias de crecimiento y seguridad, que es el conocimiento que todo líder debe poseer para; desempeñar esta importante función, ya que sin esta base sólida de conocimientos sería imposible esperar buenos resultados, y por ende sus seguidores desconfiarían en su totalidad dicha función.

Exhortamos a toda persona que tenga ese deseo ferviente de liderar, que se prepare intelectualmente, asistiendo a centros educativos donde pueda profundizarse más y mejor, participar en conferencias donde pueda alimentar este preliminar tópico, si es posible adquirir certificaciones de cualquier entidad educativa, puede ser institutos, escuelas, academias y si es posible alguna universidad, donde pueda tener un merecido respaldo personal y profesional; donde todos sus seguidores, sean partícipes de sus conocimientos, de tener la completa seguridad en quien confiar, que lo puedan imitar, que puedan seguir su valioso ejemplo, ya sea en actividades grupales o individuales, para que en un futuro no muy lejano; se conviertan sus seguidores en los LIDERES, más que la sociedad y la comunidad los necesita.

La verdad es de que a través de los servicios de crecimiento para una formación espiritual, que se frecuentan, hoy en día en todo el mundo ha sido, especialmente en las Iglesias cristianas, y donde han salido los verdaderos líderes, donde su único objetivo a lograr, es el conocer la verdad de la palabra de nuestro señor Jesucristo, que hace miles y miles de años fue establecida para la salvación de la humanidad, donde se enfoca el trabajo arduo, que nuestros pastores lo vienen realizando, donde su tiempo y trabajo entregado a formar líderes, al desarrollo de esta gran misión, en lo absoluto no son económicamente remunerados, confiando en la bendición celestial de que Jehová proveerá, para estos buenos barones incluyendo su familia total, los recursos que sean necesarios, para profundizar y acrecentar dicha obra, si bien es cierto la capacidad de preparación intelectual, en su mayoría es auto realizada por ellos mismos, ya hoy en día las cosas han cambiado, existen centros de capacitación profesional donde les ofrecen, un mejor sistema de aprendizaje, en lo que a cursos teológicos se pueda necesitar.

Y de aquí es lo que nacen los verdaderos líderes, que con su gran esfuerzo y dedicación lo han podido alcanzar, y siendo un orgullo grande para que puedan predicar el evangelio de la salvación, no obstante se puede dejar de un lado el gran legado que Jesucristo, con su brillante sabiduría, supo ser el verdadero líder que hoy,

Lo que el líder lo comienza siempre lo termina hoy y siempre.

es para nosotros el gran ejemplo que nos da el cambio en nuestras vidas, permitiéndonos el goce total, de tal manera que para ser un buen líder se necesita tener estos grandes principios, para que combinados con el aprendizaje intelectual de hoy, los resultados son los que nos mantienen en esperanza y en fe.

Mejor es adquirir sabiduría que oro preciado;

Y adquirir inteligencia vale más que la plata.

Prov.: 16:16

El conocimiento es aquel que a los líderes los han llevado a cruzar las esferas de todo el universo y hoy en día son aquellos que pueden marcar la diferencia, con el conocimiento se ha podido construir bases sólidas y tangibles que han sobrepasado el límite del pensamiento humano, es aquel que te proyecta de una dimensión a otra, construyendo el presente, modificando errores del pasado para colocarte en una proyección futura.

Esto es lo que hace la mente humana, al producir los mejores pensamientos de crecimiento, donde hoy en día los líderes se han aprovechado de esta gran bendición que nuestro creador nos pudo dar, para crear una realidad existente en la cual tu y yo vivimos.

La metafísica cuántica, también aporta sus sabias enseñanzas al desarrollo de lo que un líder lo ha podido lograr, donde nos enfoca que la mente humana, nunca está de descanso, siempre está en continuo movimiento, trabajando día y noche, produciendo pensamientos, que se trasladan a un pasado que ya no está, para pasar por un presente y desarrollar las mejores estrategias que te permitan obtener un futuro deseado.

Hoy en día la historia se pregunta cómo hemos llegado y hasta donde hemos llegado, producto de la idea, de un pensamiento desarrollado en la mente humana, y es el líder el que se hace acreedor de esta increíble pero muy verídica realidad, que un día pensó, actuó y poco a poco lo fue desarrollándolo, hasta convertirlo hoy en una realidad, para que tú y yo seamos los beneficiados en esta sociedad, ya sea desde el cuadro de Miguel Ángel hasta el último computador que lo tienes en tus manos.

LIDER AFRICANO

Tuve el privilegio de poder entrevistar a este líder africano, donde su comentario me llevo a la reflexión muy profunda de saber cómo trabajan tan arduamente, en desarrollar sus grandes proyectos, en luchar fuertemente contra el racismo, que es un problema muy atenuante, contra sus principios de raza, color, religión, política y normas de cultura, y quede de lo más impresionado, al escuchar de que no es fácil encontrarse en un mundo anglosajón donde el principal problema de crecimiento ha sido el color de su piel-negros.

Pero para este africano declarado por su comunidad como un líder ejemplar, que con su gran capacidad de liderazgo, hoy se enfrenta a los grandes retos que los pueda encontrar, motivado por su gran profesionalismo y dinamismo que a un líder lo caracteriza, el comenta de que es reconocido a nivel mundial, en su mente no hay obstáculo alguno, por ser negro que le impida donde quiera llegar.

Un gran testimonio que me exhorta a seguir estos principios de perseverancia, y de no dar mente a ningún criterio negativo que pueda en mi recorrido como líder encontrar.

El líder siempre se encuentra en medio de su masa grupal para, para controlar y dirigir su gente.

CAPACIDAD PARA INSPIRAR

Este gran componente del liderazgo, surge de la gran necesidad que todo líder debe tener, para que el que este bajo la dirección y responsabilidad de un buen grupo, pueda impartir con confianza su conocimiento adquirido y sea el verdadero líder que el grupo lo necesita, para que sus seguidores lo puedan imitar, palabra muy compleja cuando hablamos de capacidad, que científicamente es galardonada por los grandes líderes a nivel mundial, que es la base sobre la cual se puede edificar una, buena masa grupal; consciente de que para que haya una buena motivación a inspirar a un determinado grupo, se necesita la suficiente capacidad, no solo en el ámbito intelectual que de por si es lo primordial, a esto se suma, su destreza de seguir perseverando en lo planificado, una buena imagen personal, física y social ayuda a desarrollar mejor este importante tópico, aquí planteado donde cualquier líder que se sienta capaz de liderar un determinado grupo social, va a ser imprescindible de esta cualidad en su mente y corazón.

La verdad es de que hoy en día se dice ser líder, a todo aquel que en su boca se pueda pronunciar yo soy quien manda y controla aquí, me siento de lo más fuerte para poder liderar, aquí se tiene que hacer lo que yo ordene, una personalidad de un colérico poderoso, que todo lo puede y todo lo sabe, que hoy en día es lo que la sociedad nos presenta, que no tienen ni la más mínima idea, de cómo hay que liderar, se creen dueños y señores de su propio conocimiento, desencadenando un gigantesco caos en la mente del que de verdad está expuesto a saber liderar, no desarrollan un conocimiento compartido, no son dinámicos en sus actividades, les gusta a esta clase de líderes competir con otras entidades, que al final de la historia no hay resultados, que favorezcan o motiven a alguien a ejercer dicha función.

Esta capacidad de liderar, tiene que ser convincente en toda su plenitud, en la mente de él que espera liderar, ya que de ahí nace el primer ingrediente para obtener, el adecuado mecanismo de cómo ser un líder ejemplar, debemos mencionar que a esto se suma la fuerza físico, mental, intelectual e espiritual, para reforzar esos grandes deseos que se necesita para adquirir el anhelado oficio de saber liderar, que ya puestos y enfocados en la vida práctica, nunca pueden fallar, porque con honestidad, con sacrificio, con perseverancia, de conseguir lo que se desea, te llevaran hacia el pináculo más alto de tus anhelados sueños, descubrirás por ti mismo los grandes logros, que te impulsaran día a día a ser el mejor, y con completa seguridad, desarrollaras en ti, la fuerza innovadora que se necesita, para ser un líder con clase, con calidad, con destreza, con simpatía, con elegancia en el ámbito local, nacional, internacional y por qué no decirlo a nivel mundial.

El desarrollo de una buena capacidad para influenciar en un determinado grupo, será la base más importante para dejar el nombre de un líder, en lo más alto, para que sea la buena imagen y el gran ejemplo o legado a seguir por una causa digna de poderla ejecutar, con conocimientos enfocados en una existente realidad, sin vanagloriedades de la vida, no jactancias que no te confundan tu vida real, sino con el impulso que te permita ser optimista, humilde, sencillo, desarrollando los dones que JESUS, nos inculco a través de sus grandes discípulos y que hoy estos principios han llegado a revolucionar la mente de toda la humanidad.

UN LIDER NORTEAMERICANO

Desde la metrópolis para el mundo entero, el magnate de los rascacielos, en la gran manzana, DAVID SCOTT, compartió temas de vital importancia en lo que a mi investigación de liderazgo se refiere, y lo que menciono con todo respeto a este interesante tópico muy esencial en la vida de los seres humanos manifestó lo siguiente:

Todo es posible para el que quiere conseguir lo que de veras se proponga en la vida, su mente está preparada para recibir lo bueno y desechar lo malo, una gran verdad que a este gran magnate, le pudo suceder para que hoy me lo pueda testimoniar, él puso en práctica estos grandes principios y hoy goza de una vida de felicidad, exhortándonos para que imitemos, a seguir este gran legado.

Comenta que desde temprana edad siempre tuvo el gran deseo de llegar a estar entre los grandes, como todo proyecto, tiene sus grandes misterios por resolver para encontrar el correcto camino que te lleve hacia la meta, cuenta de que pudo recibir las mejores enseñanzas de liderazgo, donde miraba muy detenidamente, el correcto proceso para conseguir lo deseado, y es así que se le impregna ese gran deseo de ser un líder. Que en el transcurrir de su vida lo va desarrollando, comenta que tuvo que capacitarse, prepararse emocionalmente, espiritualmente, físicamente, intelectualmente y materialmente, para ofrecer seguridad y confianza a sus seguidores.

Y llega a la meta final, donde hoy en día es reconocido mundialmente por sus grandes conocimientos de liderazgo, su gran fortuna, sus grandes mansiones, y muchas cosas más que las ha podido conseguir, en conclusión exhortándome para que no desista de mi visión, y que un día no muy lejano también llegaran para mí.

LIDERES CHINOS

GHIENSEG AND CHAU SHIU, lideres orientales que se hacen presente ante mi investigación, con sus grandes aportes de liderazgo.

Es el trabajo la principal característica que los hace y los distingue como verdaderos líderes, su enfoque total es trabajar y trabajar, y lo más importante que esta actividad la realizan todos para uno y uno para todos, que hasta su misma vida la entregan por dedicación al trabajo, en sus mentes y corazón, siempre le dan más prioridad trabajar que a sus mismas familias, comentan que para no perder ni un solo segundo de trabajo, prefieren dormir en el mismo lugar, olvidándose por completo de que tienen hogar.

Característica muy peculiar ante los ojos de los demás, que no sucede con las demás comunidades, es menester indicar sobre las cualidades que un líder lo amerita, para esta organización oriental, se destacan por ser muy perseverantes, haciéndolos únicos en el mundo y la sociedad.

UN BUEN ESTILO E IMAGEN DEL LIDER

Aunque se lo pueda ver muy desapercibido este aspecto tiene que ver mucho en el desarrollo de un líder de calidad su presentación, que es la que impacta, ante los ojos de sus seguidores, una buena imagen y un buen estilo da mucho que pensar, son ingredientes básicos para complementar, este importante tópico de lo que se necesita en la actualidad para ser un buen líder y lo que la sociedad y el mundo entero se lo exige o cualquier institución, para desarrollar con eficiencia y eficacia el papel de ser un líder ejemplar.

Desde otro punto de vista lo podemos apreciar, a la imagen o a su forma como tiene que ser presentado en su masa grupal, influye a cabalidad, que su presentación sea muy formal, dándole una buena seriedad a su objetivo, no obstante cabe resaltar, que para ciertas comunidades grupales, como la que mencionamos con anterioridad, me refiero a la comunidad china, este aspecto que fortalece la presencia de un buen líder, lo tienen olvidado o desapercibido, que en lo absoluto para ellos no ha sido impedimento alguno que los desmotive a seguir en su gran proyecto de liderar, pero que sin embargo para nuestra comunidad y la de un centenar más, la imagen y presencia de un líder, significa en su totalidad el éxito de llegar con eficacia hacia la meta.

Es importante que tengamos muy en claro esta característica en nuestras vidas personales de tener una buena imagen y una buena presencia ante las personas y ante la sociedad, esto nos permitirá abrir puertas que nos conduzcan mas rápido, hacia nuestros objetivos.

CAPITULO TRES
CARACTERISTICAS DE UN BUEN LÍDER

Es importante dar a conocer que para que un líder pueda ser de vital importancia en el desarrollo de una entidad grupal, o de cómo ser un buen líder frente a una organización, debe poseer las siguientes características o cualidades que dicha responsabilidad lo amerita, para que en el camino a trabajar pueda convertirse en un excelente líder, no va a ser fácil, pero sí de corazón quieres conocer la verdad, te exhorto a declararle la guerra a la mediocridad, a la pobreza económica, a la miseria, a los factores que no te permiten crecer y como consecuencia de todo esto iras a parar en el campo de los derrotados o fracasados, lo que eso tu y yo no lo admitimos en nuestra mente y corazón, con estos conocimientos puestos en práctica, vamos a ser buenos líderes, para que tengamos la debida aceptación, no solo por la sociedad, sino por el mundo entero, a continuación vamos a detallar y dar a conocer las principales características, las más comunes que todo líder debe poseer, a pesar de que son muchas, pero analizaremos las más importantes.

Carisma, carácter, templanza, responsabilidad, honestidad, disciplina, trabajador, actitud positiva, optimista, altruista, discernimiento, entusiasta, amor, visión, servir, que tenga capacidad, conocimiento, sencillez, poder, inspiración, compromiso, comunicación, valentía, concentración generosidad, iniciativa, saber escuchar, pasión, solución de problemas, muy buenas relaciones humanas y personales, seguridad, autodisciplina, crecimiento y un sin número más de características que e lo hacen único a un buen líder, dentro del contexto global, que la sociedad y el mundo lo amerita

CARISMA.- Es una de las cualidades que todo líder tiene que demostrar a sus seguidores este detalle de ser carismático, que se las pueda inventar de cualquier manera para mejorar la relación entre el líder y sus seguidores, factor muy importante que influye en el desarrollo de conseguir un mejor resultado en sus objetivos, lo importante que es atraer gente que le puedan seguir a su vida, que tengan la suficiente sabiduría para poder desarrollar.

Ama tu vida

Ofrece un buen plan de trabajo

Establecer las necesidades

Ofrecer esperanzas

Llamar a un compromiso

Esperar resultados

CARACTER

EL Carácter es muy importante en el desarrollo grupal, un entendimiento total en el desarrollo de ideas y de trabajo, al desarrollar tu carácter estas expuesto a tener una buena comunicación, usando el don de hablar con todos tus seguidores, para algunos expertos en este tema se dice que es una elección muy buena para que puedas y alcances el éxito, para que puedas desarrollar un buen carácter en tu persona, desarrollando más convicción en tu área débil, debes enfrentar con valentía cualquier consecuencia para que puedas reconstruir el área afectada.

COMPROMISO

Nuestro compromiso debe ser con el corazón para alcanzar lo anhelado, desarrollando con acciones y esperar buenos resultados, una cualidad muy convincente de poder alcanzar un buen liderazgo, de tal manera que sus seguidores estén muy comprometidos con su líder y con ellos mismos.

Trabajar ampliamente para desarrollar tus capacidades

Preocuparte por el devenir de tus seguidores

COMUNICACION

Una buena comunicación te da la pauta para:

Comprender lo expresado, y aplicado a la vida de un buen líder con seguridad alcanzaras lo deseado, es la llave que todo líder usa para llegar al entendimiento, como ejemplo de todo esto podemos mencionar.

El líder toma todo complicado y lo vuelven muy simple ya que la comunicación no es como lo dicen sino como lo hacen.

Ser muy específico y claro

Muy eficiente

Desarrollar una buena credibilidad con sus seguidores

Esperar buenas respuestas de todo lo que se dice y de lo que se Hace.

CAPACIDAD

Una de las más importantes cualidades del líder para desarrollar con eficiencia es su capacidad, de estar frente a un determinado grupo de personas que lo puedan seguir, un verdadero líder se forma por su gran capacidad, ya que de esto depende que sus seguidores lo acepten y lo puedan seguir.

La verdad que todos admiramos a aquellas personas que muestran con capacidad la función de liderar, como se puede lograr este atributo:

Mantenerse al margen de mejorar

Dedícate a buscar siempre la excelencia

Esfuérzate por llegar más lejos de lo esperado

Motiva y trata de inspirar a otros.

VALENTIA

Esta gran cualidad de liderar lo impulsa hacia el deseo donde de verdad toda líder desea llegar.

Arriésgate a conseguir lo que antes no lo habías podido lograr

Esta cualidad comienza en el interior de tu ser

Trata de realizar y hacer cada vez lo mejor y correctamente sin

dejar para otro día lo que se pueda realizar hoy

Enfréntate con dignidad siempre al temor

Ser muy elocuente cuando de motivación se trata

Que tus seguidores puedan apreciar y valorar en ti los grandes

pasos y logros obtenidos

DISCERNIMIENTO

Es importante mencionar que un buen líder nunca se deje llevar por las apariencias en su vida, se desarrolla mucha inteligencia y sabiduría para poder discernir entre lo bueno y lo malo, son muy capaces de encontrar muy fácil y rápido el origen o la raíz de los obstáculos y los problemas

Tienen la grande habilidad de poder multiplicar grandes

Oportunidades de crecimiento

CONCENTRACION

Siempre su concentración es muy eficaz, persiguen un solo objetivo a la vez y con mucha facilidad regresan a los demás, desarrollándose esta gran frase de meditación donde: si persigues dos Conejos a la vez ambos se escaparan.

Concéntrate en un 80 a 90 por ciento en tu lado fuerte

Confía y trabaja por lo que quieres tú mismo

Da atención a tus prioridades

Trabaja siempre en equipo no como los que dicen llamarse jefes

que lo hacen individualmente

Concéntrate en algo específico y lograras tener efectividad

GENEROSIDAD

Que tu luz interna sea la que ilumine la obscuridad de otros

Dar sin esperar nada a cambio

Que tu mano derecha nunca sepa lo que la hace la izquierda

Considera al dinero como un recurso para poder sobrevivir

Desarrolles el hábito en tu vida de sembrar

INICIATIVA

Quien se atreve a dar un paso más con seguridad el éxito está de su lado, ya que el éxito depende mucho de la acción que tomes en tu vida, aunque vengan circunstancias adversas no podrán interrumpir tu meta, porque un buen líder con iniciativa nunca se da por vencido.

Saben lo que quieren

Se esfuerzan a diario a actuar

Siempre se arriesgan más por conseguirlo

Debemos tener en mente y en cuenta que para desarrollar una

buena e imperecedera iniciativa debemos aplicar lo siguiente:

Cambia tu actitud mental

Da ese giro que antes no lo habías hecho

Nunca esperes que las oportunidades toquen tu puerta

Da un paso más

ESCUCHAR

Un buen líder para que pueda conectarse con los corazones debe primero usar sus oídos.

El oído de un líder tiene que siempre estar conectado con las voces de los demás

Los líderes escuchan: a sus seguidores, amistades, clientes,

competidores, consejeros, familiar, oponentes y sobre todo

Siempre escuchan la voz de DIOS.

PASION

Debes disfrutar tu vida, la sepas valorar y amar, con convicción de que Dios hizo el milagro más grande en tu vida de que seas único, original sin imitación de nada, para que puedas recibir las más lindas bendiciones que Dios tiene para ti.

Es el primer paso para desarrollar cualquier proyecto en tu vida

Aumenta tu voluntad, la pasión te cambia, te transforma, hace crecer tu fe, hace de lo imposible lo posible, te da la fuerza para nunca rendirte, y para que puedas aumentar esa pasión de liderar, te exhorta que desarrolles lo siguiente:

Desarrolla el habito de bañarte muy seguido y con agua fría

Desarrolla una disciplina de mejorar tu autoestima

Relaciónate con gente optimista y muy positiva

Participa en reuniones de crecimiento

ACTITUD MENTAL POSITIVA

Si crees que lo puedes lo lograras y si no crees que lo puedes no lo lograras.

De tu actitud depende tu vida

De tu actitud depende tu crecimiento

De tu actitud depende tu felicidad

De tu actitud dependen tus acciones

Esfuérzate por ser valiente, por cambiar tu manera de actuar y de pensar bien y el mundo te podrá sonreír.

Podemos mencionar algo muy importante cuando el rey David ya moribundo le decía a su hijo Salomón, esfuérzate y se valiente, con actitud mental positiva, llegaras a conseguir todo lo que te puedas proponer en la vida.

SOLUCION DE PROBLEMAS

Dicen los grandes expertos, que los problemas en la vida son una señal de crecimiento, sino hay problemas es porque no se está progresando, es como un desierto sin oasis, es como un jardín sin flores, o tal vez diríamos que es como un hogar sin hijos, de tal manera que lo podamos entender que este tópico es inevitable en el convivir diario de nuestras vidas, debemos aceptar con valentía y serenidad, para que en el momento que lleguen, suceden dos cosas muy importantes, o nos hunden en el pozo de la desesperación o nos impulsan hacia el objetivo a alcanzarlo.

Un verdadero líder acepta los problemas con valentía

Nunca abandona la batalla

Siempre está preparado para la Victoria o para la derrota

Un líder siempre esta ahí

Cuando los problemas vienen a tu vida, con seguridad que el campo de la batalla para enfrentarlos, es tu mente, si la tienes preparada con una buena dosis de positivismo, con seguridad que salen huyendo, pero si tu mente está invadida por los dardos mortíferos del negativismo, el destino final de tu vida ira a parar en la fosa de los fracasados, así que el final solo tú eres el que decide.

Muy importante característica que se proyecta en el corazón y

mente de un líder, porque si bien es cierto hoy en día en el primer

tropezón que en encuentres en tu vida ya eres un cuento que paso

al olvido.

BUENAS RELACIONES

Las relaciones humanas de un buen líder son imprescindibles para el desarrollo de una buena organización, es el antídoto que te proyecta a cosechar grandes objetivos en una organización grupal, debes ser muy sociable, muy comunicador, llegar con un elocuente mensaje a sus seguidores, la verdad, que este factor influye demasiado en la vida de una buena organización.

Un buen líder siempre está atento con una buena comunicación en su posición

Nunca expresa inseguridad, al contrario se muestra muy seguro de su capacidad

El éxito para un líder depende mucho de una buena relación

Siempre les hace notar a sus seguidores que hay algo muy hermoso en ellos, y que lo sepan descubrir y valorar

De tal manera que si aceptas llevar el eslabón de liderar como lo hacen los grandes líderes con una muy fructífera relación y si aceptas tomar la iniciativa, llegaras a ser grande entre los grandes, llegaras a la cima del éxito, como los demás lo hicieron, esfuérzate y se valiente que la victoria es tuya.

RESPONSABILIDAD

Si no llevas la bola de juego no puedes dirigir a tu equipo, si no eres la luz que ilumina los caminos obscuros de tus seguidores no podrás ser el líder que lo anhelas, lo que trato de enfatizar es de que para ser un buen líder, tú tienes que ser el ejemplo vivo de lo que quieras lograr.

Un buen líder puede abandonar cualquier cosa pero jamás su responsabilidad

Siempre termina lo que comienza

Nunca deja para otra oportunidad lo que pueda realizarlo hoy

Siempre está dispuesto a dar más, a caminar una milla más, a esforzarse mas y mas

Son grandes motivadores por excelencia

Son muy creativos a pesar de cualquier situación que traten de desmotivarlos de su visión

Siempre aman lo que emprenden

Nunca se olvidan de los objetivos y metas a alcanzarlas y dan paso para seguir cosechando nuevas victorias, nuevos triunfos desencadenándose en ellos una eterna felicidad.

SEGURIDAD

La seguridad es la llave que te conduce a la excelencia, dando paso a que tus seguidores confíen completamente en tu palabra y en tu gran ejemplo.

Siempre sabe lo que emprende y hace lo que se debe hacer

Siempre está a la vanguardia de lo que pueda suceder, él se compromete de Corazón con sus seguidores

Nunca los abandona, ni tampoco los deja solos, el lucha por su gente

Siempre está contento, seguro, feliz de lo que hace

AUTODISCIPLINA

Con respecto a este tema, se dice que para poder cosechar una buena disciplina de tus seguidores, lo primero que tienes que hacer es disciplinarte tú mismo.

Desarrolla y cumple sus prioridades

Haz de tu estilo de vida un gran ejemplo para todos tus seguidores

Desarrolla hábitos que te proyecten a un mejor crecimiento

Aleja cualquier tipo de escusas que se te presenten o se te puedan dar

Nunca pidas por adelantado lo que todavía no los has terminado

Siempre está pendiente de sus grandes resultados.

SERVICIO

Cuando lo de siempre hazlo con amor, ya que como dice el gran proverbio del rey Salomón, el amor es el ingrediente que une todas las partes sueltas.

Un buen líder vive con amor

Entrega todo sin esperar nada a cambio

Ama a su gente más que a su posición

Da como prioridad su gran responsabilidad como líder

Tiene la seguridad y capacidad para servir

Nunca impone su posición

Vive solo por amor

APRENDER

Esfuérzate por ser cada día mejor, aprendiendo, capacitándote, el escuchar y saber leer te hará digno de ser mejor, planifica cada vez mejor tu tiempo para estar en la cima del éxito y en la paz de la montaña, cuida muy bien el momento que pasa, a lo que estás haciendo ahora, porque del hoy depende tu mañana, tu crecimiento te determinara quien eres.

Renuncia a tu orgullo y se cada vez más sencillo y así Dios te ensalzara, dándote las abundantes bendiciones ya como dice el Sabio proverbio, el que se vanaglorie será humillado, pero el que se humilla será cada vez más ensalzado

Reconoce tus errores, para que el próximo paso a dar será de mucho éxito.

VISION

Podemos enfatizar este tópico de liderazgo, que para que tengas visión, debes desarrollar tu fe, como dice fe, es la certeza de lo que se espera y la convicción de lo que no se ve

También se agrega como fe, a la fuerza de la vida, la fuerza de la inspiración, la que te permite ser visionario, no de donde estas hoy sino donde llegaras mañana

Tu visión comienza dentro de ti y te llevara hasta donde tú lo puedas ver

Te permitirá hacer realidad solo lo que tu mente pueda visualizar

La importancia que cada uno de todos los factores que fortalecen el desenvolvimiento de un buen liderazgo, hace que cada vez más, se vuelva muy importante el deseo en mí de investigar y poder encontrar el alimento que mi mente, mi alma, mi Corazón lo necesitan para ser cada vez mejor.

Estas son realidades que trabajan en el mejor de los grande caminos a elegir, por tu deseo vehemente de desarrollar tu potencialidad en lo que te proyectes con tu vida, cada cualidad y características si de verdad la pones a trabajar en tu vida personal, con completa seguridad que serás el líder de hoy y del mañana.

Nada es imposible para aquel que desarrolla y se esfuerza por ser cada día mejor, obviamente que para todo habrá que estar dispuesto a pagar el precio por alcanzar tus grandes metas y tus grandes proyectos, de tal manera que lo expuesto en este ejemplar de crecimiento, toco mi corazón, fueron las mejores experiencias vividas, para que hoy te las pueda contar de que con la ayuda de Dios, él lo hizo conmigo en un hombre de éxito y de la misma manera lo hará contigo si de verdad quieres estar donde los grandes donde hoy con la sabiduría divina y la terrenal controlan y conquistan el mundo entero.

Para poder comprender y entender mejor este importante tópico de sobre la esencia misma de la que todo líder debe ser digno de estar en el pináculo más elevado del éxito total, me he atrevido a citar con mucho respeto, a estos grandes maestros de liderazgo, con las siguientes fotos que de seguro nos fortalecerán mejor nuestro concepto de un líder ejemplar, de cómo se ven hoy en día y como la vida les ha cambiado para que sean un gran legado que tú y yo lo necesitamos para que nuestras vida puedan cambiar.

NOEMI DE MEJIA

Una mujer de Dios, entregada al servicio pastoral donde actualmente es PASTORA, de la iglesia los UNO EN CRISTO, localizada en la ciudad de Paterson NJ, ejemplo de mujer, una gran líder cristiana, nació en el evangelio, desde su temprana edad fue tocada por la presencia del Espíritu Santo, para llevar las buenas nuevas de Dios, al más necesitado, una mujer que reúne todas las características para ser considerada líder cristiana que junto con su esposo pastorean en la iglesia mencionada anterior. De origen dominicano, pastorean con profundo conocimiento y capacidad un LIDERAZGO ejemplar, llenando nuestros corazones de sabias enseñanzas, cuando escuchamos sus servicios de sanación y liberación, reconocida por su gran labor de liderar en el ámbito local, nacional e internacional.

Noemí motivada por la presencia de Jesús en su corazón, hace que el amor, la alegría, la paciencia, el gozo y todos los dones del Espíritu Santo son su eterna compañía. Una mujer soñadora desarrollando el legado de Jesús, entregada con alma, vida y corazón a las almas para su restauración.

Mujer dinámica, práctica y muy positiva, que entiende mejor los cambios dinámicos y complejos que toda mujer enfrenta hoy en día, dispuesta a ayudar en todo sentido de la palabra hasta llegar a su plenitud.

Enamorada de Jesús, fiel por su gran amor, entregada a dar su vida misma por su salvación, que hermoso legado podemos recibir de una extraordinaria mujer de Dios. Elevamos nuestras oraciones para que siga por el mismo sendero de buscar almas para Jesús, y que reciba la mejor sabiduría de nuestro Padre Celestial, para coronarla de éxitos como solo ella se lo puede merecer, Dios siga bendiciendo y cuidando a esta hermosa mujer, que hoy es coronada como un ejemplo de Liderazgo mundial.

CAPITULO CUATRO

COMO SER UN BUEN LÍDER

Tópico muy interesante para poderlo entender con un elocuente mensaje que te permita entender, como crecer en lo más importante que quieras para tu vida, para con tu familia, con tus anhelados proyectos, tu variedad de planes, todo lo que tengas en mente poder realizar, este principio con seguridad te ayudara.

Con la ayuda de Dios, se pudo investigar temas, subtemas que hablan de la materia para que lleguen a tu vida estos importantes principios, de cómo ser un buen líder en el desarrollo comunal de tu vida y a la vez te exhorto para que puedas atesorar en tu corazón esta gran verdad que viene acompañada de la correcta sabiduría y si de veras estas interesado en poner en practica estos grandes aportes para tener éxito en tu vida y puedas también ser uno de los grandes que más adelante darás aportes de liderazgo a los que lo necesitan, si estás dispuesto a seguir este gran legado, prepárate que comienza la bendición y con toda seguridad tu vida tendrá resultados que te harán ser, muy pero muy feliz.

Para ser un buen líder, no es necesario sentirte un superan, como lo dicen las historietas de cuentos del ayer, películas de fantasía donde nos han confundido nuestra mente, dándonos mensajes que en nuestra vida real, no han funcionado como desde ser, con el transitar del tiempo hemos podido madurar, y aceptar que de nuestra mente vienen los pensamientos, palabras y acciones donde construimos el mundo que vivimos muy real, que por nada del mundo nos, debemos alejar de esta realidad, este trabajo que lo he plasmado, en mi deseado libro para que pueda servir de una gran ayuda, para que tu también puedas estar de acuerdo conmigo, que para ser un buen líder dependemos de una gran capacitación y de todos los elementos y requisitos indispensables que ayuden a entender mejor, como ser el líder que tanto se lo anhela.

Los grandes expertos mencionan que para ser un buen líder se necesita ese gran deseo que salga de lo más profundo de tu corazón, en querer ser lo que anheles, ese gran deseo viene acompañado de la buena fuerza de voluntad que solamente tú eres el único en conseguirlo, nadie puede hacerlo por ti, y que mejor que estos grandes principios nos exhorten para realizarlo con dedicación, tenacidad, perseverancia, y enfocados donde queremos llegar, apuntando hacia el centro del objetivo y poder disparar las grandes flechas del amor, que conlleven optimismo y seguridad y consecuentemente obtendremos los mejores resultados deseados, para nuestro bien y de nuestras familias que nos rodean, vamos a agarrarnos de este punto para poder llegar a donde nadie lo había hecho antes, y en un devenir de los días, seremos de base edificante de una mejor vida para los que nos acompañan, seremos los grandes en llegar a las metas, nuestros grandes sueños se harán posibles, nuestros anhelos no se detendrán, ante ningún obstáculo de la vida, caminaremos con pie firme hacia la batalla, hasta donde el punto de nuestra visión nos enfoque llegar y finalmente gozaremos de estar en la cima de la montaña y en la paz del valle, que nos permita descansar en una inquebrantable tranquilidad donde nuestros seres queridos lo puedan gozar con nosotros y así tener una inmensurable vida placentera.

Es impresionante de poder apreciar el mover diario de los grandes líderes en esta sociedad, donde la crisis económica es una de las grandes trampas puestas por el enemigo para no dar paso hacia un nuevo lugar, hacia los grandes objetivos que a diario ellos sueñan como llegar, he podido apreciar desde muy cerca como los buenos líderes, se esfuerzan por ser cada día mejor, he visto que no hay obstáculo alguno que les impida seguir adelante, cuando me refiero a los grandes líderes hablo de un liderazgo mundial, líderes del medio oriente de la raza amarilla, como son los chinos en comunidad, si nos detenemos a analizar muy detenidamente, el gran secreto de estos pueblos, es de que aprovechan las mejores horas del día para conseguir lo planteado y esto es que los ha llevado a ser grandes, no pierden el tiempo en cosas efímeras, son muy concretos a la hora de la verdad, donde ellos han manifestado que donde mejor se puede percibir la mejor energía espiritual para acumular fuerzas físicas y mentales, es en el despertar muy temprano de un nuevo día, así que tuve la gran oportunidad de platicar con líderes de la raza china y su sorprendente respuesta, fue de que para ellos el trabajo es muy importante, para alcanzar grandes sueños, y a la ves pude comprobar que sus grandes seguidores de estos líderes, no se quedan atrás, van siguiendo a su fiel líder, para que en un tiempo no muy lejano puedan seguir inculcando a los que vienen atrás, como seguir creciendo en un mundo de buenas oportunidades para tener una mejor vida y personalmente me agarro de este gran legado y que a diario lo sigo aplicando en mi diario vivir.

Un buen líder demanda un compromiso con su corazón, desarrollado con una buena acción, para esperar grandes resultados y para poder comprender mejor este gran tópico donde se fomenta la realidad de un buen liderazgo, tuve la gran oportunidad de poder dialogar y experimentar, como el liderazgo se mueve y trabaja en el mundo entero.

ATREVIENDOSE A SOÑAR

Piensa en todas las cosas grandes y también en las cosas pequeñas que se han hecho realidad, por los grandes que se atrevieron a ser buenos líderes y que siempre supieron soñar, piensa por un instante en todas las personas que mantuvieron su postura como líderes, que miraron más allá de las adversidades de la vida, de las distorsiones de su medio donde se encontraban y de aquellos tiempos donde supieron dejar huella, a esto se debe agregar de aquellos líderes que se enfrentaron a los retos de la vida sin tener miedo alguno, ningún temor, por lo que les podría suceder, en sus mentes siempre estaba el gran deseo de ser grande entre los grandes, sentirse muy importantes, el deseo de poseer dinero, fama y fortuna y todos los componentes que lo hacen acreedor a un buen líder, piensa en todas estas cosas hermosas que sucedieron con estos personajes, te has preguntado por alguna vez de como está la realidad en que estás viviendo, los grandes adelantos, los grandes inventos, las buenas comodidades de las que hoy gozas, los grandes privilegios que te dan felicidad, te has puesto a pensar por un instante como es de que un avión puede estar a una altura y no suceder nada malo, o tal vez observas como un crucero con tantas toneladas de peso no se sumerge en el agua, o cómo fue que el hombre pudo sobrepasar las esferas del conocimiento para llegar a la luna, son estas tantas y miles de motivos y razones por las cuales tenemos que estar más interesados en valorar el trabajo majestuoso que estos hombres considerados LIDERES hoy nos sorprenden de una manera que no podemos entender.

A esto hay que agregar temas que lamentablemente hay personas que sueñan despiertas, son muy irrealistas, incapaces de separar su propia subjetividad de la realidad.

Hay un testimonio que lo quiero compartir, donde una persona tiene un sueño y lo comparte con su amigo, le comenta lo siguiente:

Soñé que cogía en el mar 100 truchas

El amigo le dice, serias tan amable de compartir esas truchas conmigo dándome la mitad.

Le contesta NO

Me darías la cuarta parte de las truchas

Le contesta NO

Me darías una 10 truchas

Le sigue contestando NO

Me darías unas 5 truchas

Nuevamente le dice NO

Acaso no te atreverías a darme una miserable trucha

Y le contesta, acaso no eres digno de soñar por ti mismo y dejar de depender del sueño de otra persona.

Una moraleja que nos exhorta a que debemos soñar por nosotros mismos, nadie puede darte soñando por ti, no esperes caer en el remolque de un tren y ser arrastrado por otro, comienza a soñar por ti mismo.

Muchos de nosotros no estamos conscientes de las partes débiles o ciegas que tenemos con respecto a nuestro comportamiento con la vida, del poder que tenemos dentro de nosotros de poder crear esa fuerza positiva que nos permita cosechar lo deseado, de poder descubrir que con nuestra fuerza positiva conquistaremos lo anhelado que hay en nuestro corazón.

ESTAS DISPUESTO A SER LIDER

No lo tomes a la ligera esta disciplina para tu vida, ni tampoco retrocedas al lugar donde empezaste, debes reconocer cuando es que tienes que prestar oídos a las palabras de los sabios, entregando tu corazón para recibir la sabia doctrina del éxito, y saber reconocer cuando estas errado para enmendar lo equivocado que con completa seguridad, será de impulso hacia lo mejor.

Nada es fácil en la vida, todo toma tiempo, saber tener mucha paciencia, como el agricultor espera su tiempo para saber cosechar, este adagio nos revela la mejor intención de cómo enfrentarse a los embates de nuestra existencia.

Acepta el gran desafío de crecer, de saber madurar, de tener en mente de que fuiste creado para edificar tu vida y la de los demás, enfréntate con valor y coraje a las pruebas que tienes que pasar y si es posible las represiones que tengas que escuchar, porque solo aquel que presta oídos a los sabios, podrás ser el hombre entendido, y hallaras gracia ante Dios y de los hombres que habitan sobre la faz de la tierra.

Si no aceptas este proceso del que te estoy hablando, serás considerado como un bebe, que no crece ni tampoco llegaras a la madurez total, no obstante que hay que reconocer que para que un bebe, pueda llegar a tener un crecimiento, estará dispuesto a soportar las diferentes caídas, que lo fortalecerán hasta que obtenga su posición de progreso en la vida de este ser. De la misma manera sucede con el líder cuando se enfrenta a su crecimiento, las caídas lo llevaran a saber perseverar y consecuentemente al destino total, donde solo el podrá marcar la diferencia.

Que es lo que quieres: el éxito o el fracaso?

Estas dispuesto a pagar el precio para llegar al éxito, quieres recibir la herencia de los grandes maestros, de los líderes, de nuestro señor Jesucristo, la voz de Dios, entonces comienza a trabajar hoy mismo por esos sueños, por tus planes que tienes con tu vida, por el proyecto que quedo olvidado, y estar listo para enfrentarte en la gran batalla, donde el enemigo se te pondrá muy resistente, tratando de hacerte renunciar a todo lo que tengas en mente hacerlo realidad.

El éxito demanda de ti, mucha responsabilidad, de saber identificar lo deseado en un presente continuo, de no aplazar para un futuro no cierto, lo que puedas realizar hoy, identificarte con tus habilidades y destrezas que te permitan acelerar tus metas, ya sea para corto plazo o largo plazo, eso está en tu mente y corazón, no desmayes ante las adversidades de la vida, piensa por un momento que ya estas donde querías estar, para que seas motivado hasta encontrar la corona donde fluye la leche y miel.

El fracaso no necesita condición alguna, para llegar a él, solamente olvidarte de lo expuesto anteriormente y lo demás te llegara sin nada que tengas que hacer. Que para el hombre de éxito y el verdadero líder este tema de fracaso es descartado, y echado a lo más profundo del mar, o enterrarlo en un pasado que no aparezca nunca más.

Una de las características por las cuales el ser humano hoy en día no llega a concretar sus sueños hecho realidad, es de que una área de su vida no está funcionando bien, algo mal o grave le puede estar aconteciendo, pueda ser su vida familiar, espiritual, de salud, emocional, física, psicológica o puede ser otra más que solamente tú la puedes identificar, que importante es saber reconocer cuál de estas es, para que entres en un momento de reflexión contigo y con Dios, usando la debida oración, ya que a través de esta encontramos paz para nuestra alma y alimentamos nuestro espíritu, nos conecta directamente con nuestro Creador y dando paso para estar en sintonía con el espíritu santo todos los días de nuestra vida y pedir dirección y poder encontrar la mejor solución, a todos los problemas y por ende el éxito estará de tu lado. Te exhorto para que apliques este principio en tu vida y veras que los resultados marcaran tu vida para siempre.

DESDE MASACHUSSETS

Compartiendo como el progreso y adelanto de esta importante ciudad, donde los miles y miles de residentes de este hermoso lugar, gozan a plenitud de su majestuosidad y hospitalario lugar, que ha sido gracias a la tangible y sólida decisión de los lideres, que incansablemente lucharon y trabajaron con dedicación, por ver hecho sus grandes sueños, una gran realidad, haciendo la cordial invitación para que todo aquel que tenga en mente venir, serán los huéspedes de honor, que Dios los bendiga y cuide de este paradisiaco lugar por siempre.

DESDE PHILADELFIA

Dios con su gran amor y poder dio luz verde, a estos grandes líderes que se inspiraron con todo su corazón, para entregarnos una ciudad desbordante de amor e hidalguía, y se complementa el verdadero oasis con vertientes que apuntan, al progreso y edificación de hacer realidad tus merecidos sueños, donde sus fieles residentes, no encuentran otra ciudad muy igual, como la llaman "MY PHILY", que sienten que hasta el aire que respiran sabe a grandeza de los lideres, que Dios siga cuidando y protegiendo este paisaje y encanto, como lo muestra la bella ciudad de PHILADELPHIA, para que si algún día decides visitar, no será tiempo perdido.

Consciente de que mi tiempo puesto en la investigación de mi libro titulado para Ud. "COMO SER UN BUEN LIDER", reúna la mejor respuesta ante cualquier inquietud o interrogante que se te pueda presentar, y tengas como fuente de consulta estos tópicos que de alguna manera te puedan dar, la pauta o la gran iniciativa que estabas esperando, para dar el primer paso de fe, y que ahora mismo puedas desempacar del baúl de los recuerdos, esos grandes deseos de buscar el éxito, los anhelos, las metas y sueños que solamente tú sabes dónde están, y con mucha paciencia y tenacidad, déjame decirte con todo mi corazón, que los podrás hacer realidad en el nombre de nuestro glorioso JESUS.

POESIA DE UN LIDER

Soy un buen líder

Óiganme gritar

Soy único en mi mundo interior

Para expresarlo en el mundo exterior

Para no ser nunca ignorado

Por ser sabio, inteligente y muy humilde

La sabiduría nace del dolor

He pagado con el precio

Por ser fuerte, invencible, soy un líder

Muchas veces derrotado pero no destruido

Más decidido por alcanzar nuevas metas

Caigo y nuevamente me levanto

Los problemas son el gran impulso

Que me conectan con un mañana mejor

Mírame de pies a cabeza

Mientras me lanzo a lo desconocido

Por el camino largo y estrecho

Hasta hacer que mi alma y mi mente entienda

Que soy un líder que nunca se rinde

Ante las adversidades de la vida

Porque tengo una luz que brilla dentro de mi

Que solo vivo para dar amor

Hoy te extiendo mis brazos

Y una sonrisa de aliento

Porque soy un líder

Óiganme por favor

Oh, líder! Soy líder! Soy líder!

Guido Rafael vaca

REGLA DE ORO

La fuerza, el poder y el conocimiento están en las manos del que todo lo puede, Dios y está listo para extendernos sus manos.

REGLA DE ORO

Quiero vivir mi vida para ti, muéstrame el mejor camino, enséñame a reconocerte como mi único Salvador.

REGLA DE ORO

Para todo el que cree, es posible desarrolla, con amor esa fe que te hará grande.

REGLA DE ORO

No importa lo que me esté sucediendo, pero mis alabanzas jamás se detendrán, proclamando tu grandeza mi señor JESUS.

REGLA DE ORO

Que hermoso eres mi JESUS, que traes a mi vida gozo para compartir con los seres que más amo.

REGLA DE ORO

Estoy en tus manos padre todopoderoso, y con mis manos abiertas te entrego mis necesidades, mientras tú asumes con amor mis grandes aflicciones.

GOD BLESS YOU

Printed in the United States
By Bookmasters

T0207948

Saved by Grace

We Can Overcome Obstacles in Our Life

APRIL UPHOLD

WESTBOW®
PRESS
A DIVISION OF THOMAS NELSON
& ZONDERVAN

WestBow Press books may be ordered through booksellers or by contacting:

WestBow Press
A Division of Thomas Nelson & Zondervan
1663 Liberty Drive
Bloomington, IN 47403
www.westbowpress.com
1 (866) 928-1240

ISBN: 978-1-4908-2159-7 (sc)
ISBN: 978-1-4908-2158-0 (hc)
ISBN: 978-1-4908-2160-3 (e)

Library of Congress Control Number: 2014900084

Printed in the United States of America.

WestBow Press rev. date: 01/15/2014

Contents

vii
Acknowledgments

ix
Introduction

Chapter 1   1
Life in the Delta

Chapter 2   25
Life in Chicago

Chapter 3   37
Back in the Delta

Chapter 4   41
Another Apartment

Chapter 5   45
Max's Concerns

Chapter 6   49
Welcome Home Again

Chapter 7   53
Max's Secrets

Chapter 8   65
Strings of Harassment

Chapter 9   73
Being Depressed

Chapter 10   81
Breaking Point

Chapter 11   87
Regaining Her Life through Christ

Acknowledgments

I give thanks to God first.

For their helpful comments, support, and encouragement, I would like to thank Keyanton Stewart, Sheldon Lee, Bryan Stewart, Brandon Stewart, and Brittany Stewart. Special thanks to Bryson Stewart and all the people that helped make this possible.

Introduction

A young lady named Silver Lay was a college graduate. She was having a difficult time getting a job that she really wanted. She worked as a substitute teacher and tax preparer in her hometown of Indianola, but she always wanted to leave her hometown and go to the city and accomplish her dreams. She believed things would really be better for her in the city. She thought she would get the kind of job that she always wanted and make the kind of money she always dreamed of having. She wanted very much to be able to take care of her small family. She wanted to live the American dream by getting a decent-paying job, but obstacles were always present. She struggled through many of her obstacles and finally accomplished her dream.

CHAPTER 1

Life in the Delta

One summer day, Silver Lay was talking on the telephone as she sat on the porch of her home in a small community called Southgate. She shared the home with her four-year-old daughter, Danielle, as well as her oldest sister, Earnestine. Up the street about six houses to the right lived her other sister, Sugar. Her sister Money lived one block south of Sugar. About eight blocks north lived her brother Woodrow.

Woodrow would always come to their house before work and eat dinner. It was as if Earnestine was cooking just for him. Once he finished with his meal, he would prepare to leave for work. It never failed that before he left for work he would always kiss someone on the forehead. I never knew why he did that. I can only imagine that this was his way of thanking them for the meal that he had eaten. I can still hear those words echoing in my mind: "Come on and give me some sugar." Silver Lay's four-year-old daughter was the recipient of most of his kisses because she would be standing by the door upon his departure. He would pick her up and kiss her on the forehead, and then he would leave for work. I can only imagine that this must have made his day, because he did this for several years.

Right after Woodrow left for work one day, Sugar pulled up in her new Oldsmobile that she had bought from the filling station. Sugar blew her horn at Silver Lay and parked the car in the driveway. Silver Lay then hung the telephone up and asked Sugar to get out of the car and come on in. So Sugar did just that and came in and spoke to Earnestine and Silver Lay's daughter. Sugar is the type of person who always jokes around, and that day was no different. Silver Lay started dressing her daughter while engaging in a conversation with Sugar. Sugar asked Silver Lay, "Are you sending Danielle to a ballet recital?" meaning the child's clothes were too tight—skin tight—and looked like something a ballerina would wear. They all laughed.

Earnestine looked at Sugar and said, "You must not have checked the mirror before leaving the house this morning, because you are a lady, but look at how tight your clothes are— skin tight." They all laughed again and continued to enjoy each other's company. They sat around joking for a little while longer, and then Sugar decided to go to the hospital.

She turned and asked Silver Lay if she would go to the hospital with her to visit their cousin. Silver Lay agreed to go with Sugar, while Earnestine agreed to stay home with Silver Lay's daughter. Silver Lay and Sugar went out and got into her new Oldsmobile and headed to the hospital.

As they entered the hospital and started walking toward their cousin's room they could not help but to notice this tall, slim, handsome, well-groomed young man. He appeared to be in his twenties. He approached them and then proceeded to introduce himself to Silver Lay and Sugar as Max. He went on to tell them that he was from Florida and was down here visiting his aunt, who was in the hospital. Sugar introduced herself and then introduced Silver Lay as her baby sister.

Sugar let her introduction reflect that they were locals from right there in the Delta. Sugar and Silver Lay then turned with big smiles on their faces and, looking each other straight in the eye, mouthed the word "Max." They quickly turned back around and said, "Welcome, Max, to the Delta." Max thanked them and went on to tell them about his aunt, whom he was visiting in the hospital. The young ladies said that they were visiting their cousin, who was also in the hospital, and they thought they would bring a little cheer to him. At that moment it seemed as though a light bulb came on in Max's head; he opened his eyes wide and suggested that they visit each other's relatives and bring cheer to both his aunt and their cousin. Silver Lay and Sugar thought that was a great idea, so they quickly agreed.

They walked to his aunt's room and knocked on the door, and his aunt asked them to come in. When she saw that it was family, she was very happy. Max introduced Silver Lay and Sugar to his aunt Sail. After he introduced them, they all started talking about how his aunt Sail was doing and when she would be released from the hospital. She replied, "I hope very soon." Sugar told Max's aunt Sail that she hoped that she would feel better soon, and she also told her to have a good day. Aunt Sail said to come back again. They all said good-bye and started walking down the hall to visit Silver Lay and Sugar's cousin.

They stopped in front of their cousin's room and knocked on the door. They heard his voice when he said, "Come in," and they entered his room. Sugar introduced Max to their cousin Rex. Max said, "I am pleased to meet you," and Rex reciprocated the greeting.

After being formally introduced, Max turned and asked Rex if he knew when he was going to be released from the hospital. He said, "Tomorrow, man, and I can't wait to be released from this place." Silver Lay and Sugar asked their cousin whether he needed them to do anything for him before his release. He replied, "No, not at this time, but I am glad to see you all." It was getting late in the day, and they all had other things to do, so they told their cousin that they would call and check on him the following day to make sure that he had been discharged. He then told them to have a safe trip home.

As the three of them were leaving Rex's room, Max asked Sugar and Silver Lay if they would like to have dinner with him. They were both surprised, and Sugar replied, "I ate before I left home." Silver Lay stated that she had another engagement.

Max replied, "Maybe another time."

"Yes, maybe another time," said Silver Lay.

Max went on to ask Silver Lay for her telephone number, and she gave it to him. Max then walked them to the exit of the hospital and said good-bye. Silver Lay and Sugar left for home, but not until Sugar showed off her new Oldsmobile. Sugar drove to her sister Money's house and blew the horn. Money came out and said, "Hey, guys, I almost didn't know who you were in that sharp Oldsmobile."

Sugar said, "I had to get this Oldsmobile so I could stay off my feet." She went on exaggerating about how red her feet had been when she used to walk. They all laughed.

After talking with Money for a while, Sugar told Money that they had to leave but they would talk to her later. Sugar dropped Silver Lay back off at home and told her that she would see her later, and then she drove off.

Silver Lay's daughter was glad she had returned and showed it by greeting her mother at the door with a big hug and a kiss. Silver Lay and her daughter walked into the kitchen, where Earnestine was cooking dinner. Silver Lay said, "What is this I smell cooking?" It smelled so delicious. Earnestine said, "That's rib-eye steak."

Silver Lay replied, "How much longer before dinner?"

Earnestine said, "Not much longer, because dinner has been on for a while."

Silver Lay and her daughter went to their room. Silver Lay sat in the old rocking chair with her daughter on her lap. She began reading her a story called *The Cat in the Hat*, which was her daughter's favorite book. As she read the book, she watched Danielle as she fought to keep her eyes open, and then at last she fell fast asleep. After laying Danielle in the bed, Silver Lay returned to the kitchen to talk to her sister, who was still cooking. They started a conversation about Sugar and her new Oldsmobile. They were both happy that Sugar had finally been able to afford a new car. Silver Lay told Earnestine that she might have to leave Mississippi in order to find a decent-paying job.

In the midst of her last statement, the telephone rang. They both turned, looked at each other, and wondered who could be calling on the telephone since neither of them was expecting a telephone call. Silver Lay got up and answered the telephone and was surprised at the voice she heard on the other end, especially since she hadn't expected to hear it again. It was Max's pleasant voice. "Hello," he said, "May I speak with Silver Lay?"

Silver Lay replied, "This is Silver Lay."

"How is the family?"

"They are fine."

Just two days after meeting Silver Lay at the hospital, Max asked again to take her to dinner. Silver Lay replied, "Maybe another time."

Max said, "Okay," and started a conversation about how his aunt was doing and how her recovery was going. He also said that if she kept progressing, she would be released soon from the hospital. He told Silver Lay that he would be returning to Florida within the next three days. Silver Lay wished him a safe trip, and they both said good-bye.

After hanging up the telephone, she then called her best friend, Cotton, and told her that she had met a guy from Florida that she thought was cool and who was handsome, slim, and tall. Cotton asked Silver Lay, "Does he have a cool brother?"

Silver Lay replied, "The next time I talk to him, I will ask him."

Silver Lay and Cotton soon changed the subject and started talking about their children. Cotton stated that she was going to purchase her son a pair of shoes, and Silver Lay said that she was going to purchase her daughter a dress.

Cotton then replied, "When you go to town I want to get a ride with you." Silver Lay said the best time to go to town would be on the weekend. Cotton agreed because they both had jobs as substitute teachers. Cotton then told Silver Lay to let her know what time she was going to town so she could be ready. Cotton reminded Silver Lay to ask Max if he indeed had an equally charming brother. They both laughed and then hung up. They both were barely making ends meet. They were best friends who could relate to each other's situations because the only income they had was from their jobs as substitute teachers and Silver Lay's part-time job as a tax preparer's assistant. Silver Lay was hesitant, but she really wanted to leave Mississippi and go to the city so she could find a decent job to support her small family.

Earnestine yelled through the house, "Dinner is ready." Silver Lay then awakened her daughter, who was taking a nap, and went to the bathroom to clean up for dinner. On the way down the hall, Silver Lay yelled, "That steak must be calling me; it smells so good."

Earnestine said to Silver Lay, "You are not the only person that steak was calling; look who's coming in the back door— Woodrow." Earnestine then said to Woodrow, "Just come on in, and I'll serve your food." Silver Lay served her and her daughter's food. They had rib-eye steak with carrots and potatoes diced around it, brown-n-serve rolls, peach cobbler for dessert, and a large, cold glass of iced tea to wash it down.

Earnestine served Woodrow and herself, and they all ate. They are a traditional family, and they believe that the women should serve the men's food. Silver Lay complimented Earnestine on the meal. "Girl, you must have put your foot in this meal."

Earnestine replied, "Thank you, thank you, dear." Then Woodrow gave Danielle her usual forehead kiss and left for work.

(Sometimes Danielle would stand by the back door so she could be the recipient of his kiss.) Silver Lay then put up the leftovers and washed the dishes before retiring to the living room.

Silver Lay turned the television on, and their favorite movie was on—*The Beverly Hillbillies*. Silver Lay said to Earnestine, "One day I am going to strike it rich like those Hillbillies."

Earnestine replied, "Strike it rich! Don't forget about your sister when you get rich."

"You will be the first person that I remember.

"Okay girl," said Earnestine; then they both laughed. When the movie ended, they decided that it was time for bed.

Early the next morning, while everyone was still in bed, they heard the telephone ring. It was Max; he had been in Florida for three days. He said, "Hello, may I speak with Silver Lay?"

Silver Lay replied, "This is she." She was wondering when he would begin to recognize her voice. He told Silver Lay that he liked Florida but didn't have any family out there and missed not having family around him. He then told her that he would be moving to Chicago soon because he wanted to be closer to his sisters and brother. Silver Lay agreed that this would be a great move for him to get closer to his family.

Max then changed the topic of the conversation from himself to Silver Lay and her daughter. He told her that if she would allow him to, he would take care of her and her daughter. He also told her that she wouldn't have to work unless she wanted to and that her daughter could go to private school if she accepted him as her man. Silver Lay was speechless for a moment, and she then told him that she would definitely think about it. It all seemed very unreal to her since they had known each other for only a few days.

They then said good-bye and hung up. Silver Lay sat in shock for a few moments, wondering if Max would be a nice, faithful man if she were Max's woman. She thought, *Maybe I will give him a chance.*

Silver Lay couldn't call him back, because she did not know his telephone number. In fact, he had never given her his telephone number. Max really flattered her, but she also wanted a second opinion about the situation with Max. Silver Lay picked up the telephone and called her friend Brittany and started talking about how charming and handsome Max was. She told her that Max said he wanted to take care of her and her daughter. Brittany replied, "Go for it, girl; what do you have to lose? You're already struggling; how bad could it be?" Silver Lay felt joy in her heart; all she had wanted was to hear someone else to say what she was thinking.

Silver Lay decided to get Earnestine's opinion about Max, as Earnestine was her oldest sister. She went to Earnestine's room and asked Earnestine, "What if a man says he fell in love with you at first sight and wants to take care of you and your daughter?"

Earnestine said, "Are you talking about the guy you and Sugar met at the hospital?"

"Yes."

"I have to be honest with you," said Earnestine, "I don't believe in love at first sight. I personally feel that a woman and man should take their time to get to know each other and then see if they have feelings for each other."

Silver Lay then turned to walk out of Earnestine's room. Earnestine told her that she hoped she had not hurt her feelings but that she was giving her true opinion of how love should be approached. She also told her that she only wanted the best for her. Silver Lay walked out of Earnestine's room and went to her room and went to bed.

The next morning, Earnestine got up and began her normal house cleaning routine. Once she finished cleaning the house, she began to cook dinner. This time she decided to cook neck bones, turnip greens, and lemon cake, and she made iced tea. Silver Lay soon got up and did her part of the cleaning. In the back of her mind, she was contemplating whether or not she should have a relationship with Max. After all, she had not known him that long.

In the midst of her thoughts, the telephone rang. It was Max. She answered the telephone, and he asked Silver Lay, "Will you be my wife"? He had finally recognized her voice across the telephone. Max had changed the question about starting a relationship to one of marriage. Silver Lay thought this was fast. She told Max that she would start a relationship with him and think about being his wife later. Max told Silver Lay that she would never forget the beautiful relationship that they would have.

Silver Lay asked Max to call her back later because she had some things to do with her daughter. Instead of saying good-bye when the conversation ended, Max said, "Love you." After Silver Lay hung the telephone up, she took her daughter outside to play. Silver Lay sat on the porch as her daughter played in the front yard with a large beach ball.

Penny Line, Silver Lay's neighbor, saw Silver Lay sitting on the porch and came over to join her. They started talking about Silver Lay's daughter and the fun she was having with the beach ball. Penny Line said to Silver Lay, "The ball is bigger than your daughter."

She replied, "I know; I just thought it would be fun for her to wrestle with." Silver Lay and Penny Line laughed as her daughter rolled and wrestled with the beach ball.

Penny Line told Silver Lay that she was going in the house to talk with Earnestine. As she walked into the house, the telephone rang. Penny Line answered the telephone, and on the other end, a young man asked to speak to Silver Lay, so Penny Line passed the telephone out the door to Silver Lay. She said hello, and it was Max on the other end. He asked Silver Lay again, "Will you marry me?"

Silver Lay thought he was joking, so she said yes. He told her that he would bring the engagement ring on his way to Chicago. He asked her what size ring she wore. She told him she wore a size ten.

Max assured Silver Lay that he really meant that he was going to take care of her and her daughter because he was a gentleman. He said to her, "The men in Mississippi have been playing with you." They both laughed.

Max said, "I will call you tonight, okay."

Silver Lay said, "Okay."

They both hung the telephone up. She called her daughter to the porch and said "Let's go eat." They went inside, where Earnestine and Penny Line were. Silver Lay asked Earnestine, "Is dinner ready?"

"Yes," said Earnestine.

Silver Lay and her daughter washed up and made it back to the kitchen. Earnestine asked Penny Line to stay for dinner. Penny Line said, "No thanks, I just finished eating before I came over here, and now it's time for me to leave. Enjoy your meal." She then walked out the door and back across the yard toward her home. Silver Lay and her daughter were ready to eat, so they sat down with Earnestine. With every mouthful, they boasted about how good the food was. After they finished, Danielle wanted more lemon cake. Silver Lay gave Danielle a second serving of cake.

Woodrow walked in the kitchen door and said "What's that I smell?"

Earnestine said, "Just wash your hands and get a plate." He opened the top cabinet, got a plate, and handed it to Earnestine. She handed his plate back to him with everything on it. Sometimes I believe Earnestine was cooking for Woodrow.

He sat down and ate his food fast. As he was eating, he said, "I don't have a lot of time. I've got to get to work. He ate in a hurry and walked out the door. He swiftly looked behind him and saw Danielle standing in the doorway waving good-bye. He knew right then that he had not kissed her forehead. He ran back to the back door to kiss Danielle, and then he said good-bye. He got into his old Chevrolet truck, and off to work he went.

Silver Lay got up from the table and started cleaning the kitchen. Penny Line knocked on the kitchen door. She asked Silver Lay to drive her to the store. Silver Lay replied, "I will drive you as soon I finish cleaning the kitchen."

Earnestine said, "Bring some ham hocks for dinner tomorrow."

"Okay," said Silver Lay.

Silver Lay and Penny Line left to go to the store, leaving Danielle with Earnestine. As they drove to the store, they saw Sugar; she had run out of gas in her new Chevrolet. Silver Lay asked Sugar, "What's the problem, girl? Have you been riding too much?"

Sugar just laughed and said, "I am getting ready to ride again."

On their way into the grocery store Silver Lay and Penny Line glanced at Sugar as she went past. Silver Lay and Penny Line both retrieved shopping carts and went their separate ways in the grocery store.

After thirty minutes had passed, they met up at the checkout counter to pay for their purchases. Once they finished paying, they carted their purchases off to the car and drove back home, where Earnestine was waiting for the ham hocks. When Silver Lay gave Earnestine the ham hocks, she decided to go ahead and precook the meat for dinner the following night. Earnestine liked to cook. Penny Line thanked Silver Lay for driving her to the store and walked back across the yard to her house.

As Silver Lay unpacked the groceries, the telephone rang. It was Max. He was letting her know that he had finished packing everything and that he was making his transition to Chicago to be closer to his family. He said he thought it would be best to move around his family, and Silver Lay agreed. He also told Silver Lay that he would be leaving Florida in a few days, headed to Chicago, and he wanted to stop in Indianola where she lived to give her an engagement ring. Silver Lay agreed that he could bring the engagement ring to her. Max said, "I'll see you in a couple of days."

"Okay," she said, and she hung up.

Silver Lay returned to the kitchen to finish unpacking the groceries. Earnestine asked her, "Who was that on the telephone?"

She replied, "It was Max; he's moving to Chicago in a few days and wanted to know if he could drop off the engagement ring that he promised to give me."

"Please tell me that you did not tell that man you would marry him. I hope that you are not going to accept this engagement ring from someone that you really don't know. You really don't know his background or anything about his people."

Silver Lay said that she was not serious about marrying him and really didn't think he was serious about marring her. She just wanted to wear an engagement ring and show it off to her friends.

Silver Lay got on the telephone and called her friend Cotton. She bragged about how she might be getting engaged and maybe married later. She just wanted to see what her best friend thought about the situation, although she was just joking about marrying Max. Cotton thought it would be a good idea for Silver Lay to get married. Cotton told Silver Lay that she was happy she had found someone that wanted to take care of her and her daughter, and she was really serious about it. That was what Silver Lay wanted to hear. They said bye and hung the telephone up. The next day, Silver Lay decided to talk with Penny Line to see what she had to say about her being engaged to a concerned, handsome, and charming young man who said that he was going to take care of her and her daughter. Penny Line said that sounded nice and that she wanted to meet this man.

Penny Line went back over to Silver Lay's house and sat in the kitchen with Earnestine and Silver Lay. Silver Lay told Penny Line that Max said he would be bringing her an engagement ring in a few days. She went on to tell her that he would be moving from Florida to Chicago to be close to his family. Penny Line said, "I am not impressed that Max will be bringing you an engagement ring, because you are a very nice person with a pleasant attitude, and I am sure Max has picked up on that." Earnestine said that she was too nice to date someone that she really didn't know much about.

Earnestine was cooking pinto beans and ham hocks. Penny Line asked Earnestine, "What you are planning on cooking with those pinto beans and ham hocks?

Silver Lay said, "Those pinto beans and ham hocks smell so good."

Earnestine told Penny Line that she was going to cook cornbread and banana pudding. Penny Line said that sounded as though it was going to be a good dinner.

Penny Line turned and looked at Silver Lay and said, "Well, it's your life, and you will have to make this decision."

Silver started all over again, telling Penny Line that this handsome man from Florida said that he wanted to take care of her and her daughter.

Penny Line looked at Earnestine, and Earnestine looked at Penny Line, and Penny Line said, "Well, I hope he is as nice as you think he is."

Penny Line got up from the table and headed out the back door and across the yard to her home. Earnestine yelled out the back door, "We'll be outside later, girl!"

Silver Lay took her daughter to their room to read her a book—*The Cat in the Hat.* Just as she finished reading, Earnestine called for them to come eat dinner. They washed up and went to the kitchen to eat. Silver Lay served herself and her daughter while Earnestine served herself. They then sat down to eat. After they finished eating, they went outside to watch Danielle play with her beach ball. Penny Line came back across the yard to sit with Silver Lay and Earnestine. They watched Danielle play in the yard until the sun went down.

Penny Line got up and told them that it was getting late and she was going in for the night. Penny Line walked back across the yard to her home. Silver Lay and Earnestine decided that they would go in for the night too. They were surprised that Woodrow hadn't shown up for dinner. They knew that since he had missed today, he would definitely be there on time the next day. They turned the TV on and started watching their favorite movie, *The Beverly Hillbillies.* When the movie was over, they took their bath and went to bed.

The telephone rang; it was Max, calling to let Silver Lay know that he would be arriving in Indianola the next day around twelve o'clock. Silver Lay told Max that she would be expecting him at that time. Max said, "Good night and sweet dreams," and then he hung up. Silver Lay soon after went to sleep.

Silver Lay slept late the next morning. She was awakened when she heard the horn of a car. She looked out the window and saw Max being dropped off by a cab service. She was expecting him at twelve o'clock, but he arrived at eleven o'clock. His bus had arrived early. Silver Lay jumped to her feet and hurriedly put on her jeans and top so that she didn't have to keep Max waiting outside. When she opened the door, Max was standing there with the engagement ring and wedding ring in his hand. He placed the engagement ring on her finger and asked her again, "Will you marry me?"

Silver Lay suggested that they first get engaged before actually making that big step of marriage. Max agreed.

Penny Line raced over to see if everything was okay, because the loud honking of the horn had awakened her. Silver Lay replied, "Everything is fine; it's just Max. He arrived early."

Silver Lay asked Penny Line to come in the living room so she could introduce Max to her. Silver Lay introduced Max to Penny Line. Max said, "It is a pleasure to meet you." Penny Line returned the greeting.

Earnestine heard the talking in the living room and decided to come see what was going on. Silver Lay turned and said, "Earnestine, this is Max, and he is on his way to Chicago to live near his relatives."

Earnestine asked, "Where are you moving from?"

Max replied, "Florida, which is a nice place to live, but I missed my family and decided to move back home to Chicago."

Earnestine told Max that she was glad to meet him and that she hoped he enjoyed his visit.

Max looked at Silver Lay and said, "I am sure I will."

Danielle finally got up and came down the hallway to the living room, where everyone was gathered. Max said, "You must be Danielle, the little one that I have been hearing so much about."

Silver Lay said, "Yes, this is my precious little daughter, Danielle."

Max looked at Silver Lay and said, "I'm sure that Danielle and I will get along just fine."

Max told Earnestine that he had heard about how much she liked to cook, but today he wanted to treat them to dinner. Silver Lay said, "That sounds good to me; we all can go in my car." Earnestine told Max that she was sorry but would have to pass on the invitation because she had another engagement. Penny Line then turned and said that she would love to go since she didn't have anything planned. Penny Line went home to freshen up while Silver Lay and Danielle did the same.

Earnestine stayed in the living room with Max. She asked Max, "What time are you planning on leaving for Chicago?" He stated that he was leaving right after dinner because he was so anxious to see his siblings again.

As Penny Line walked back into the house, Silver Lay and Danielle were coming into the living room to leave for dinner with Max. Max said, "I finally get the chance to take you out for dinner. I have been trying to get this date ever since I met you at the hospital." Everybody smiled and walked out the door to Silver Lay's car. They all got into the car so they could go for their dinner in Greenwood. Greenwood was only thirty minutes away from Indianola, and Max wanted Silver Lay to drop him off at the train station after dinner so he could be on his way to Chicago. Silver Lay thought that it would be best for them to go to Greenwood because that was the closest town with a train station.

Upon their arrival in Greenwood, Max saw a Holiday Inn and asked Silver Lay if she would park in the parking lot. He told them that they would be dining at the restaurant in the hotel before he left for Chicago. They walked into the hotel restaurant, and everything was lavish and glamorous. Silver Lay thought Max could not afford the dinner. When the waiter came to their table, Silver Lay and Penny Line only ordered hamburgers and fries, as that was the cheapest meal on the menu. Max noticed that they were not eating a full-course meal. He assured them that he had the finances to pay for their food, that it was not a problem for him to pay, and that they could order whatever they wanted to eat.

After everyone finished eating, Max walked over to the counter and paid for the meals with his back to Silver Lay and Penny Line as though he was trying to hide something from them. After he finished paying for the meals, they all got up and headed for the door. Silver Lay knew that her next destination was the train station to drop Max off.

They arrived on time for Max to catch the eight o'clock train to Chicago. Max walked into the train station and purchased a ticket. Silver Lay, Danielle, and Penny Line waited outside. When Max came out, he talked to Silver Lay and told her that once he was settled in Chicago he would send for her and Danielle. It was soon time for Max to board the train, so they all said good-bye. Silver Lay and Penny Line turned and walked to the car so they could go back to Indianola. It had been a long day for them.

On the way back home to Indianola, Silver Lay reminisced about her life and told Penny Line that she had graduated from college and still lived with her older sister. She kept talking, telling Penny Line that she couldn't even find a decent job or the kind of job that she wanted. She said that she was tired of substitute teaching at the neighborhood school and that she needed more than substitute work to take care of her family. She went on to say that if Max got a job and a place to live, she would likely go to stay with him so she could find a job to help take care of her daughter. "I know that Max and I have not known each other for a long time," she said, "but I really do like him, and I feel like I would have a better chance of getting a job in the city than in a small town."

Max kept in touch with Silver Lay while he was in Chicago. Sometimes he would call three times a day. Silver Lay couldn't understand how Max was making so many calls from a pay telephone. She enjoyed his conservation and was really getting interested in him more and more each day. Max called to inform Silver Lay of all of his good news. He told her that he had found a job at a clinic downtown working as an orderly. He also told her that he had an apartment and he wanted her to come live with him in Chicago.

Silver Lay didn't answer, so Max said again, "Will you come live with me in Chicago?"

Silver Lay was speechless and silent for a moment. She replied, "I will think about it." They both then hung up.

Silver Lay started thinking about her goals for her family and that she wanted a job that paid a salary that she and her small family could live on. Before making a final decision, she went to talk with her oldest sister, Earnestine. She wanted her input on moving with Max, whether or not she would take what Earnestine said seriously.

She discussed the idea about moving to Chicago with her sister Earnestine, and as always, Earnestine gave her honest personal opinion. Earnestine didn't think it was a good idea, but she left the decision up to Silver Lay.

Later that day, Max called and asked Silver Lay if she had made up her mind.

"Yes," she said.

"Well, don't keep me in suspense; what is your answer?"

"I decided to give it a try. I will move with you to Chicago."

The next day, Silver Lay began packing her and Danielle's clothes to make the transition to Chicago. They would be leaving the following day. Earnestine was in the kitchen cooking greens, fried chicken, cornbread, and tea cakes and making iced tea. Silver

Lay really didn't want to leave Earnestine, and Earnestine really didn't want Silver Lay to leave, but Silver Lay was thinking about her future.

Silver Lay's mind was constantly thinking about all the good and positive things that were to come for her. She was thinking that after she got there and found a job, she would ask Earnestine to come live with them. Or, if Earnestine decided that the city life was not for her, then she would send Earnestine money to help take care of her. She would even send enough money so Earnestine could go shopping.

When Silver Lay finished packing her and Danielle's clothes, she came to the kitchen to eat dinner. When she sat down to eat, Woodrow came to the back door and said, "Girl, did you put your foot in this meal? I can smell it outside." As usual, Earnestine told him to get a plate out of the cabinet, and she fixed it for him and told him to sit down and eat. He said on the double, "I'll sit down and eat this good food any day of the week."

Sugar and Money were riding in the neighborhood and saw Woodrow over at Earnestine and Silver Lay's house. They stopped and came in and started poking fun at Woodrow. Sugar said to Woodrow, "I see why your stomach is as big as Danielle's beach ball." They all laughed.

Penny Line walked through the back door and said, "What are you guys doing, having a family gathering? You didn't invite me."

Earnestine said, "Since you all are here, you can say bye to Silver Lay and Danielle. They are getting ready to leave and go to Chicago."

Sugar said, "It's about time she got out from under your dress tail."

Silver Lay said, "I am going to try living in the city for a while to accomplish some of the things that I really want. If for any reason I don't like it, I know my way back home."

Everybody in the house told her that she was right and that she should go do her thing.

Soon the guests left and Silver Lay went back to finish packing while Earnestine cleaned the kitchen. After they finished, they went outside with Penny Line to watch Danielle play in the yard with her beach ball. They sat outside until the sun went down. Penny Line then walked back across the yard to her house.

Silver Lay, Earnestine, and Danielle stayed for a few minutes longer and then got up and went inside the house. Silver Lay decided that she would go to the bus station to purchase their bus ticket for tomorrow. She asked Earnestine to come alone, so they all left for the bus station located on highway 49. Silver Lay went inside and purchased the bus ticket. She came back out with the tickets in her hand. Earnestine looked at her and said, "So you are really leaving."

She replied, "Yes, but it's just for a while."

They returned home, got out of the car, and went into the house to watch another episode of their favorite show, *The Beverly Hillbillies.* Silver Lay knew it was going to be a long trip to Chicago. She read her daughter a bedtime story and put her to bed early.

Max called Silver Lay as she was tucking her daughter into bed. He wanted to know what time the bus was leaving Indianola tomorrow because he wanted to be at the bus station in Chicago on time to meet them. She told him that the bus would be leaving at eight o'clock the next morning. She and her daughter were scheduled to arrive in Chicago at eleven o'clock the next day. He assured her that he would be at the bus station waiting for them. They said bye and hung up.

The next morning, Silver Lay got up early and woke her daughter up for the long trip to Chicago. They showered and got dressed. Silver Lay left her car with Earnestine and called a cab to take her and Danielle to the bus station. The cab arrived in less than fifteen minutes. They hugged Earnestine and said good-bye. They got into the cab, and as Earnestine waved good-bye, the cab drove off.

They arrived at the bus station about ten minutes before the bus arrived. When the bus parked and opened the door, they boarded the bus, making sure to get a window seat. Silver Lay and Danielle were on the bus all day. The bus driver had to stop in several Mississippi towns to pick up passengers on their way to Memphis, Tennessee. When they arrived in Memphis, they had to brace themselves for a two-hour layover. The layover seemed more like five hours, but needless to say it finally ended and they got back on the bus. They arrived in Chicago at eleven, just as scheduled.

CHAPTER 2

Life in Chicago

The bus parked in the terminal, and everyone started exiting the bus. Silver Lay and Danielle stepped off the bus, and there was Max, waiting with open arms, walking toward them. He hugged them and welcomed them to Chicago. After the warm greeting, he grabbed their luggage and they all walked toward the CTA bus stop to catch the bus to his apartment.

After arriving at Max's apartment, Silver Lay found that he was living a lifestyle quite different from the one she had anticipated. The apartment was a one-bedroom basement apartment with dim lights, one sofa, one bed, and a dirty floor. Silver Lay thought his place would only be suitable for rats to live in. Silver Lay asked Max, "Why did you get such an apartment?"

He told her that he had quit his job at the clinic. Silver Lay wanted to know the reason he quit his job, and he told her that the manager had wanted to pay him less money than the other orderly was being paid. She was curious about what Max was saying, and deep in her heart she wanted to believe him, but at the moment the only thing she wanted to do was clean the apartment so she could cook and feed her daughter so they could get some rest after the long trip.

Silver Lay started thinking that Max had seemed to have everything a woman wanted or needed from a man when he came down from Florida to Indianola. He was handsome, charming, and trustworthy—or so she thought. Now he seemed to be one of the poorest and most pitiful men in Chicago. Silver Lay asked Max to show her the clinic where he used to work as an orderly. Max turned his head and told her that he would show her tomorrow.

They both got warm water, soap, and bleach to clean the apartment. They dusted and cleaned the sofa and bed. After a great deal of work, the apartment was finally clean, and Silver Lay went to the kitchen and started cooking Hamburger Helper and toasting bread while Max and her daughter watched TV. When the food was ready, she fixed their plates, and they all sat around the coffee table and ate.

Once they had finished eating and placed the dishes in the sink, Silver Lay and Danielle returned to the living room to watch a movie while Max washed the dishes. When he finished, he joined Silver Lay and Danielle in the living room to watch the movie. After the movie they had been watching ended, they were off to bed for the night.

In the middle of the night, they were awakened by a noise that sounded like somebody running across the apartment floor. When Max turned the light on, there was a big wood rat running in the bedroom where they were. Silver Lay jumped straight up in the bed, screaming and holding her daughter in her arms. Max then got up and started setting traps all over the apartment. When he finished setting the rat traps, he came back to bed and assured them that everything was all right and that they could lie down and go back to sleep.

They did lie back down and finally went back to sleep. They didn't stir until around seven in the morning, when they were awakened by the smell of food; Max had gotten up and cooked breakfast, trying to make amends for the previous night. After finishing their breakfast, they got up and got dressed because this was the day they were to go meet Max's family. They walked to the CTA bus stop to catch the bus to his sister Robbie's house. When they arrived at Robbie's house, his other two sisters, Leach and Macy, were there also. They all talked about the times when they used to live down south in the town of Clarksdale. They made comparisons between Clarksdale and Chicago. They talked about how the weather was much better in the south and how the food was better there too. They went on talking about the weather and how the temperature in the city of Chicago during winter was always below freezing. Robbie decided that it was snack time, so she served everyone snacks, and Danielle played with Robbie's children. They all had a great time.

Max decided that it was getting late, and Danielle was getting tired, so he told Robbie and his other sisters that they had to go, but not before reminding Robbie that they would be calling on her to babysit Danielle while they looked for work. Robbie agreed to watch Danielle anytime. Silver Lay, Max, and Danielle then left Robbie's house and walked back to the CTA stop to catch the bus back to their apartment.

On the way back, Silver Lay asked Max again to show her the clinic where he once worked. Max told Silver Lay that the clinic was closed and the building had been leased to another company. Silver Lay thought that was strange, but she accepted his explanation. When they arrived at the apartment, Danielle was sleepy, so they put her to bed for a short nap as they watched TV.

On Monday, Max and Silver Lay got up and got dressed to go look for a job. They rode the ATM train out to Robbie's house so that she could watch Danielle until they were done job searching. They had an idea of where to look, because they had found some job openings in the newspaper want ads. They rode the CTA bus south because this was the direction in which the job vacancies were all located. They even went to places out south that they hadn't found in the newspaper. They searched well into the evening. Whenever they finished filling their applications out, the managers seemed to always say, "We'll get back with you." They were exhausted, and it was getting late, so they caught the train back to Robbie's apartment to pick up Danielle.

When they arrived at their apartment, Silver Lay took out Danielle's toy box so she could play with her toys while she and Max rested on the sofa. After about thirty minutes, Silver Lay got up from the sofa and fixed supper. They ate and got dressed for bed.

Every day, they would get up and go through the same routine. They stated to each other that they would take any minimum-wage job. The one thing that they definitely did not want to do was become welfare recipients.

Max started leaving Silver Lay at home with her daughter, and he kept looking for a job. He began riding the CTA bus out west to fill out job applications. He also started going north. As months passed, no one called either of them for an interview.

It finally came to the inevitable; Max decided that he would ride the CTA bus to the welfare office to apply for public assistance. He walked in the door and signed his name on the register. Soon one of the caseworkers came to the front and called his name. Max got up and followed the caseworker to the back, where her office was located. She asked Max some questions, and he answered to the best of his ability. After the caseworker finished asking questions and filling out the paperwork, she told Max that she had to take the paperwork to her supervisor to peruse. Max sat patiently waiting for her return.

After being out for about ten minutes, she walked back into her office and told Max that her boss had approved his application and that he would start receiving emergency funds within the next week. Max thanked the caseworker for her service, walked out the door and went to the next block, and caught the CTA bus back to the apartment.

When Max arrived back at the apartment, he starts telling Silver Lay about how he had gone to the welfare office to apply for public assistance and that he would start receiving emergency assistance within the next week. He also told her that the caseworker said that he would begin receiving his regular monthly payment of $145 and $135 in food coupons at the beginning of the next month. Max went on to say that the rent was coming up, along with other bills. They both agreed that finding a job had not been easy for them. Silver Lay decided to ask Max if he would take her to the welfare office so she could apply for food coupons.

The next morning, they got up bright and early to go the welfare office. They arrived at the welfare office about eight o'clock that morning, and Silver Lay walked to the desk and signed her name on the register that read "Food Coupons Only." Then she sat down and waited patiently for her name to be called. Finally the caseworker came to the front and called her name. Silver Lay got up and walked to the back, where the caseworker's office was located. The caseworker asked her some questions and asked her to sign the application for food coupons only. The caseworker told her that she would take the application and other paperwork to her supervisor so she could peruse it, and that once she had finished perusing the paperwork, the caseworker would let Silver Lay know the supervisor's decision.

When the caseworker returned, she told Silver Lay that she did qualify for emergency food coupons and would be getting them the following week. The caseworker went on to tell her that she would receive monthly food coupons in the amount of $345. Silver Lay thanked the worker, and she and Max got up and walked out of the office. They headed back to the CTA bus stop and caught the bus back to the apartment. Max told Silver Lay that it was not much, but she had to start somewhere.

As they entered the apartment, the telephone rang. It was someone from a sales office calling for Silver Lay to come in for an interview at eight the next morning. Silver Lay hung the telephone up and start screaming to Max, "I got one, I got one, I got one!"

He replied, "Got one what"?

"A job interview."

"Where?"

"At the sales office on Sixty-Third and Stony Island."

They got their best sparkling water out to celebrate. They both gave a toast for the interview. Silver Lay started cooking supper while Danielle and Max continued to watch TV. When she finished, they ate and got ready for bed.

They woke about five the next morning to get dressed so that they could catch the CTA bus to Robbie's apartment to drop Danielle off to play with Robbie's children. Then they were off to Silver Lay's interview. They boarded the train to Sixty-Third and Stony Island and walked across the street to the building in which Silver Lay's interview would take place. Silver Lay was dressed casually for an interview, while Max was dressed in snow boots. As they approached the door to go in, the doorman let Silver Lay through the door but placed his arm out so that Max couldn't enter the building. He told Max that he could not come in the building with snow boots on. He even went so far as to laugh at Max's snow boots. Max got very upset and retaliated by making a snowball and throwing it at the building. He finally made up his mind to walk down the street to a warm place to wait on Silver Lay while she was being interviewed.

While inside the building, Silver Lay saw Keyton, one of her associates from Indianola. She gave Keyton a big hug and asked how long she had been in Chicago. Keyton told her that she had been there for about two years. She said that she had been looking for a job for about two years and had been very unsuccessful. Keyton had finally been called for this interview, although she didn't believe that she was going to accept this job.

At that point, a young man called all the potential employers to the back of the building. He asked them to have a seat and watch a film on selling Hoover vacuum cleaners door-to-door. He gave them a brochure on Hoover vacuums to see the kinds of Hoover vacuums they would be selling. When the film was over, he asked how many would be interested in this job. Two people raised their hands. He said, "Well, good day to the rest of you," and those who hadn't raised their hands got up and left.

Silver Lay saw Keyton again outside the building and went over to chat with her. She began telling Keyton that she had only been in Chicago for a few months and had been to a lot of places looking for work. She also said that she had thought that once she moved to the big city she would be able to find work easier than in a small town. Keyton assured Silver Lay that it was not easy finding a decent job in the city. After their conversation about jobs, Silver Lay saw Max standing down the street waiting for her. She wished Keyton well, and Keyton wished her well in return. They both walked away.

Silver Lay started walking down the street toward Max. They met, and she started telling him about the interview and how disappointed she was about the company wanting them to sell Hoover vacuum cleaners in the ice and snow. She told Max that she had not accepted the job. She explained that she didn't even have a car in which to transport vacuum cleaners. He told her that she did the right thing, and they walked back to the CTA bus stop where they caught the bus to Robbie's apartment to pick up Danielle.

When they arrived at Robbie's apartment, Silver Lay began to tell Robbie about the job interview. She told her that it was for a job selling Hoover vacuum cleaners door-to-door and that she didn't have a car in which to carry vacuum cleaners. She went on to tell her that she had not accepted the position. Robbie replied, "I wouldn't have accepted the position either. There's too much ice on the ground, and it's ten below freezing."

Silver Lay said, "Girl, I really don't want to apply for the money from the welfare office."

Robbie replied, "You might have to until you get what you are really looking for."

Max said it was getting late and they needed to get back home. They got Danielle and went to the CTA bus stop. They boarded the bus and went back to the apartment. Silver Lay fixed supper, and they all ate. When they finished, they watched a movie on the TV. Danielle fell asleep while the movie was still on. Silver Lay watched the movie until it ended and then got up and dressed Danielle in her night clothes so she could put her to bed before she went to bed herself.

The next morning, Silver Lay got up and got dressed. Silver told Max that she had no choice but to ask him to take her to the welfare office again so she could apply for the money payment to help support her daughter and the apartment. She thought that with just Max's welfare coming in they would not have enough to take care of all the payments they owed. Max, Silver Lay, and Danielle went to the CTA bus stop and boarded the bus to the welfare office. They got off and went inside. Silver Lay signed up to receive welfare money payments.

She went through the same routine as before. A caseworker called her to the back and asked her some questions, and she signed the application. Then she took the application to her supervisor to have her peruse it. After the supervisor finished perusing the application, the caseworker returned to her office to inform Silver Lay that she would receive her first money payment on the first of the month.

Within a month, Silver Lay did receive her first money payment. She and Max went to the currency exchange to cash the check and to get the funds to pay their utility bills. They were content living in the one-bedroom apartment until one of them secured a decent job.

Just when Silver Lay thought there were no more problems in the apartment, one night they were awakened by a wood rat running across the bedroom floor again. Silver Lay jumped straight up in bed, holding Danielle in her arms while screaming. It seemed as though it had missed the rat trap and had just been running around in the apartment. Max got up and went into the kitchen and moved the trap to where he thought the rat was coming in. He then told Silver Lay that they could go back to sleep, which they did.

When they awakened the next morning, Silver Lay decided to tell Max that they could no longer live in that apartment. She decided that she and her daughter were moving back to Indianola until Max found a decent place to live. Silver Lay called her sister to have her wire her some money to purchase tickets back home for her and Danielle. Her sister asked what the problem was and she told her that Max had gotten a basement apartment and wood rats were coming in. Earnestine told Silver Lay that she would wire the money to her that day.

Silver Lay started packing their bags to leave for Mississippi. The next day, Max rode the CTA bus along with Silver Lay and Danielle to the Greyhound bus station. He watched them and waved good-bye as they boarded the bus to Mississippi. Silver Lay and Danielle waved back as the bus drove away from the terminal.

CHAPTER 3

Back in the Delta

They had a long ride and slept half the way home. When they got to Indianola, they called for a cab to come to the bus station and take them home. Earnestine and Penny Line saw the cab dropping them off and ran to the door to welcome them back home. They ran and hugged each other. Penny Line helped carried the luggage inside. Before Silver Lay could sit down, Penny Line wanted to know where Max was and how she had been. Silver Lay said that she had been doing well but couldn't find a job and had to get on welfare.

Silver said that she had thought the big city was where one could see all the movie stars and the bright, glittering lights. She was disappointed because they had lived in a one-bedroom apartment that was infested with rats that came out at night. She told Penny Line that the only way she would go back to Chicago was if Max found a nice apartment. Silver said, "You look well, so I know you've been doing well." She told Penny Line and

Earnestine that she and Danielle were going to change into some comfortable clothes.

At that time the telephone rang; it was Max wanting to know if they had had a safe trip back to Indianola. She told him that they had made it back safely and that everyone was doing well. He asked her to tell everyone that he said hello. After Silver Lay and her daughter changed clothes, they went back up front, where Earnestine and Penny Line were. They all went outside to watch Danielle play with her ball. Silver Lay said it was just like old times. They sat out until late evening. When they went into the house, it was time for Danielle to take her bath and get ready for bed. Silver Lay and Earnestine watched the *Beverly Hillbillies*. When the show ended, they both went to bed.

The next morning Max called Silver Lay. He told her that he missed them very much and that he was still looking for an apartment. Silver Lay replied that she missed him too but that she and Danielle couldn't live in that apartment. He promised her that he would have a better place in one month. She stated that she was looking forward for it. They said good-bye and hung up.

Silver Lay went into the kitchen, where Earnestine was cooking. She told Earnestine that Max had called and promised that he would have another apartment within a month. Earnestine asked Silver Lay if she believed him. For some reason, Earnestine just didn't believe in Max.

After a month went by, Max called one Monday morning to tell Silver Lay that he had found an apartment and that now they could come back to Chicago. She started thinking that he was a man of his word, but at the same time she was questioning him. She asked, "Is the apartment in that same building?"

"No."

"Is the apartment better than the other one?"

"Yes, yes, yes. Now tell me when you're coming back."

Silver Lay replied, "I'll leave Friday night."

"Then I will be waiting at the bus station Saturday night." With that, they hung up.

Silver Lay went to tell Earnestine that Max had told her he had found a better apartment and that they could go back to Chicago. Earnestine asked Silver Lay what she was going to do. Silver Lay said, "I am going to Chicago this weekend, but can I leave my daughter with you?" Earnestine said that would be okay.

Silver Lay explained to her daughter that she would be leaving that weekend to go back to Chicago and that she wanted her to stay with Earnestine. Danielle was happy to stay with Earnestine, and Earnestine was happy that Danielle would be staying with her. Danielle ran to Earnestine and hugged her tightly. Silver Lay said, "I knew I wouldn't have anything to worry about."

CHAPTER 4

Another Apartment

Silver Lay left for Chicago Saturday morning, but she really felt bad about leaving her daughter behind. She knew in her heart that she had to check this apartment out before she brought Danielle to live in it. She started thinking about how the apartment that she was about to go to might look. She thought, *Maybe it's nice like he said, and maybe it's not.* All of a sudden, she drifted off to sleep.

When she awoke she was in Memphis, Tennessee. She had to stay in Memphis for the next two hours, so she took a seat at the bus station and started watching TV. Time went by quickly. She noticed an announcement saying that the bus to Chicago was ready for boarding at gate twelve. She immediately got up to get on the bus.

Soon she was headed to Chicago, the Windy City. When she arrived in Chicago, there stood Max with open arms, ready to take her to the new apartment. They walked to the CTA bus stop and caught the bus to the same neighborhood, but a block over. Max had rented a second-floor apartment from a woman named Mrs. Give Moor on that block. Max said, "The more you give Mrs. Give Moor, the more she wants." Why he said that, she didn't know, so she asked Max what he meant by that. He told her that Mrs. Give Moor's name fit her personality, because he paid her what she said she wanted for rent, but as he walked down the staircase she asked for a few dollars more. He said Mrs. Give Moor was greedy for money and that's why her name fit her character.

All Silver Lay wanted was a clean apartment, and this apartment was much cleaner than the other one. The only issue was that they had to share the bathroom with another tenant. The tenant was a lady that was always intoxicated. She would leave her dirty clothes in the bathtub and wash them the next day or two days later. She drank Wild Irish Rose every day. Silver Lay couldn't understand why she was intoxicated every day. Max said, "That is what most people in the city do."

When Silver Lay finished unpacking, she heard a train go by. She looked out the window and saw a train traveling by the second floor. She thought it was unusual for a train to be off the ground. Just to get out of the apartment for a while, Silver Lay asked Max to walk her to the nearest pay phone so she could call Earnestine and let her know that she'd had a safe trip back to Chicago and tell her the location of the apartment and all about the train that passes the apartment. Earnestine was glad to hear from Max. Silver Lay told Danielle that she missed her, and Danielle told her the same. Silver Lay then hung the telephone up and went back to the apartment with Max.

That night, it seemed as though the train passed by every four hours. They finally went to sleep and were later awakened by the train. The train made a lot of noise, and when it passed the apartment building, the building shook. Silver Lay went back to sleep, but the train passed by again, making so much noise that it caused her to jump straight up in bed. She thought it was the end of the world. Silver Lay wanted to tell Max that they had to begin looking for work so they could get an apartment in another area, but she really didn't want Max to think that she didn't appreciate what he had already done.

Christmas came, and snow was on the ground again. It was cold, and the wind chill was so low they could barely go outside. Silver Lay wanted to go back to Mississippi to be with her family, especially her daughter, for Christmas. No buses would be traveling for the entire week because of the weather conditions. She called her sister to let her know that she would not be coming home for Christmas but that she would mail her gifts. Max and Silver Lay went out to buy gifts to send back home to Danielle and Earnestine. When they finally finished shopping, they went to the post office to have the packages delivered before Christmas

A week passed by before Max and Silver Lay could get out in the weather to call Earnestine and ask her if they had received the gifts. Earnestine told Silver Lay that Danielle was enjoying her gifts. Earnestine put Danielle on the telephone to tell her mother that she enjoyed the gifts. She also told her mother that she loved her. They wished each other a merry Christmas and a happy New Year, and then they hung up. Max and Silver Lay walked back to the apartment, where they had supper and went to bed.

The next morning they got up and got dressed to go look for a job. They didn't have any luck. They went back to the apartment.

They decided to wait until winter was over before they started looking for work again.

They lived by a regular routine. Every morning they would get up, eat breakfast, watch TV until suppertime, and then go back to bed. And when necessary, they would go to the currency exchange to pay bills. Springtime finally came, and Max and Silver Lay began looking for jobs. They filled out applications at many places in Chicago. Silver Lay filled out applications in Mississippi and Chicago, and Max filled out applications for security guard jobs in Chicago.

CHAPTER 5

Max's Concerns

One morning Silver Lay called home to see how her daughter and Earnestine were doing. Earnestine told Silver Lay that her daughter was ill and wanted to be with her. Silver Lay did not hesitate at all about her daughter's illness and getting back to Indianola. She told Max that her daughter was ill and she needed to use some of the money that they had saved for bills. Max replied that she could use as much as she needed to go home to be with her daughter. Silver Lay boarded the eleven o'clock bus to Indianola the same day.

She arrived in Indianola at twelve the next day. She called a cab, and the cab drove her to Earnestine's house. She walked through the door without knocking, because the door was never locked during the daytime, and she hugged Earnestine and asked, "Where is my daughter?" Earnestine told her that she was napping in her bedroom. Silver Lay ran to the bedroom and embraced her daughter in her arms. Her daughter woke up and started kissing her mother on her cheeks. Silver Lay decided that she would stay with her daughter until she recuperated from her illness. Max called every day to check on her and her daughter.

Max was very caring. He wanted Silver Lay to be with her daughter while she was not feeling well. He called the next day to insist that Silver Lay bring Danielle back to Chicago. Silver Lay told Max that she was going to take Danielle to the doctor in Mississippi and stay with her until she start feeling better.

Max called the next evening to find out what the doctor had said was wrong with Danielle. She replied, "She is doing fine; it's just a cold." He suggested that she bring her daughter back to Chicago again. She thought that would be a good idea. Silver Lay nourished her daughter back to good health.

While Silver Lay was in Mississippi, Max got a call for a security guard position and secured the job, so he had the funds to send for Silver Lay and Danielle. After another week passed, Silver Lay told Earnestine that she and Danielle were going back to Chicago. Earnestine said, "If that is what you want, then I agree."

Silver Lay had been in Mississippi for more than two weeks taking care of her daughter. She decided that Danielle was up to making the trip back to Chicago. Silver Lay packed Danielle's clothes and called the bus station to see when the bus was leaving for Chicago. She was informed by the ticket seller that they had a bus leaving Friday evening at 7:45 p.m., scheduled to arrive in Chicago at 9:45 a.m.

On Friday Silver Lay and her daughter boarded the seven forty-five bus to Chicago. When they arrived, they were extremely tired and asked Max to take them to the apartment so they could get some rest. When they arrived at the apartment, they went to bed. They didn't even wake up through the night.

The next morning, Max went to work. Silver Lay and her daughter got up and got dressed. They ate breakfast and started watching TV. soon it was time for Max to get off work. Danielle went to the window and looked for him. Max came up the steps. He saw Danielle in the window and asked Silver Lay to make sure that she didn't look out the window anymore because a little girl had just been shot down the street while looking out the window. Silver Lay assured Max that Danielle would not look out the window again.

Later that day, the neighbor's daughter came over to ask if Danielle could come out to play with her. She said that her mother would watch them. Silver Lay told Danielle that she could go play and that she would be watching them also. Danielle and the neighbor little girl went down the steps holding hands as Max and Silver Lay looked on. She and the neighbor little girl started hopping and jumping up and down and clapping hands on the sidewalk while singing nursery rhymes.

They played for about thirty minutes before Max walked down the steps and told Danielle that it was time for her to come in. Silver Lay cleaned Danielle up for supper, and they all ate. Max got a call from his job asking him to work a double shift. He said they needed the money, so he left for work. Silver Lay and her daughter got dressed for bed, and while in bed, Silver Lay decided that she would watch TV since she was not sleepy.

All of a sudden, she heard someone rattle the doorknob. For a minute she thought it was Max coming back into the apartment. Silver Lay got up to answer the door but remembered that Max had a door key, so she and her daughter stood waiting for him to enter, but no one came in. Then they heard the doorknob rattle again. Silver Lay remembered that Max had told her to go see Mrs. Give Moor in the upstairs apartment if she had any problems while he was at work. She grabbed her daughter by the hand and ran straight up the stairs.

She didn't realize that Mrs. Give Moor had dogs around her apartment. The dogs began barking unstoppably. She turned and ran back down to her apartment. She noticed that no one had been in her apartment. She assumed that when Mrs. Give Moor's dogs started barking, they must have scared the intruder away. She was exhausted and wanted to go to sleep. She got Danielle ready for bed, and then she got herself ready. They fell asleep in minutes, only to be awakened by Max standing over them. Silver Lay jumped up in bed and started to tell Max what had happened. He told her that no one would come in that apartment because Mrs. Give Moor had too many dogs. Max did look around, but he didn't find any sign of breaking and entering.

Silver Lay told Max that she wanted to move out of that neighborhood. She wanted to move south. She decided to take Danielle down south to live with her sister again until she found work. Max agreed that she could do so. She wanted to help Max find an apartment down south and help out on the income.

CHAPTER 6

Welcome Home Again

Silver Lay and Danielle caught the bus on the upcoming weekend and headed to Indianola. They arrived in Indianola at eight o'clock Saturday morning. A cab driver was at the bus station, ready to take people to their destination. Silver Lay and Danielle got in the cab and rode to Earnestine's house. Earnestine and Penny Line were glad to see them. They all hugged and went inside to catch up on the news in Chicago. Silver Lay took Danielle to her room. They would always have a room at Earnestine's house.

Silver Lay came back to the front of the house and sat down to start telling Earnestine and Penny Line about life in the windy city. She said life was great there and she wanted to live there, but in another area. She said that living close to downtown was not a good area for her and the family. She was bringing Danielle home so she could look for work to help Max find an apartment down south. She liked that area and wanted to live close to Lake Michigan. She asked them, "What's been going on in the south"?

Earnestine said, "I've been doing the same thing—getting up, cooking, and cleaning, and most of the time Woodrow comes over and eats dinner with me.

Penny Line said, "I still come over and sit outside and inside with Earnestine."

Max called to see if Silver Lay and Danielle had had a safe trip home. Max told Silver Lay that he was going to take care of her and that he wished she had stayed in Chicago, because he was still looking for an apartment down south. Silver Lay said that she didn't want him to bear the entire burden. She wanted to help out too. They said good-bye and hung up.

Penny Line was glad to see Silver Lay. She gave her a big hug and said she would come over later to sit outside with them. They said okay, and Earnestine went to the kitchen to start cooking dinner while Silver Lay went to check on Danielle. Silver Lay didn't come back up front, so Earnestine decided she would go check on them. They were fast asleep. Earnestine thought they must have been tired from the trip.

She went back up front to continue cooking. She was cooking cabbage, cornbread, and fried chicken, and she made iced tea. After she finished cooking, she called Silver Lay and her daughter to come eat. They washed up and came to eat and saw Woodrow at the door with a plate in his hand. He told Earnestine that he didn't have time to sit down and eat because he was running late.

Earnestine hurriedly fixed his plate, wrapped it, and handed it back to him. Woodrow turned to go to his truck and thought about kissing Danielle on the forehead before he left. After he kissed Danielle, they all wished Woodrow a blessed day and finished their meal.

A week passed. Max called Silver Lay to tell her that he had found an apartment down south on Stony Island. She was so glad that she could finally live where she wanted to live. He said to her, "When you get back, we are going to go purchase the furniture." He also told Silver Lay that she didn't need a job, because he would take care of her and Danielle. Silver Lay thought that was nice, but she didn't think he had that kind of income. Max even went to the point of asking Silver Lay if she thought Earnestine would like to come and stay a while with them. Silver Lay said that she would ask her. They said good-bye and hung up.

Silver Lay turned to Earnestine and asked, "Would you like to come to Chicago with me? Max would like for you to come. I will really need a babysitter if I find a job."

Earnestine said, "Oh, well, okay." They went outside to call their neighbor, Penny Line, to let her know that Earnestine was going to Chicago with her that coming Saturday. Penny Line told Earnestine that she was going to miss her company every day and asked her not to forget about her when she got to the city with a smile on her face. Earnestine replied that she would never forget about her. Then Earnestine said that she would not stay in Chicago long.

CHAPTER 7

Max's Secrets

Silver Lay and Earnestine went to their dad's house to let him know that they would be leaving for Chicago Saturday and to ask him to check around the house while they were out of town. He assured them that he would check around the house and gave Silver Lay his Amoco gas card to purchase gas on the way to Chicago. He told Silver Lay that he was glad she was leaving the small town of Indianola They said good-bye and left for home. When they arrived at home, they called Sugar, Money, and Woodrow and told them that they were leaving for Chicago. They all wished them well on their trip.

On Saturday, Silver Lay, Earnestine, and Danielle left for Chicago at 2:00 a.m. Saturday. They made a stop at an Amoco gas station to purchase gas and food. They arrived in Chicago at three o'clock Sunday evening. When they drove to the apartment, Max was standing outside with open arms to greet Silver Lay, Danielle, and Earnestine. Earnestine said that Max was too friendly for her.

She said, "There's something about him that I just can't put my finger on."

They all got out of the car and went inside. They sat at the table and started talking about how hard it was to find a job. Silver Lay said she had been looking for a job for over a year and hadn't been able to find one. She told the others that she sometimes thought about moving back to Mississippi and just trying her luck there again. Max said it had taken him a half a year to get a job. He had been with the company only a half a year, and they were thinking about laying their employees off.

Earnestine changed the subject by saying she wanted a ham. Max stated that he would get her one.

Max and Silver Lay walked to the supermarket to buy a ham. They entered the store, and Max was walking slightly behind Silver Lay. Inside the store, he was still walking behind Silver Lay. She thought it was a little strange for him to stay behind her. They walked to the meat department of the store, but before she could say "Let's get this ham," Max said, "Let's go."

They approached the door to leave. Silver Lay heard a security guard say, "Hold it right there, sir."

She looked back and saw the guard looking right at Max. She started to tremble in her knees because she knew he was talking to Max, but Max didn't stop walking. He walked right past Silver Lay. When Max was about to exit the store, the security guard pulled his coat, causing Max to drop a ham from under his coat to the floor. Then Max started running. As he was running, he invited the security guard outside for a fight. He yelled back into the store, telling the security guard to come outside and fight him. He really wanted to fight the security guard. The security guard called for backup, and Max ran. Max was acting like a wild man. This was the part of him that Silver Lay had never seen.

Silver Lay left the store walking in the opposite direction of the way Max ran. When she got back to the apartment, Max was standing outside, waiting for her to arrive. She asked him, "Why did you try to steal a ham?" She thought that he had the money to buy a ham.

He replied, "I didn't have any money, but I thought I could get away with stealing a ham for my favorite sister-in-law."

Earnestine asked Silver Lay what had happened to Max. She went on to ask her sister if he had been drinking. Silver Lay said she didn't know what had gotten into Max. Earnestine replied, "Well, that man is going to get you and him in trouble." Silver Lay agreed, although she still thought her sister was a little overprotective of her. Silver Lay's sister always wanted the best for her and never wanted to see her hurt.

Earnestine always kept an open mind when it came to Max. The next day, Max and Silver Lay drove to Popeye's to pick up a chicken dinner for supper. The car's engine was cutting out at every corner. They finally got there and back with the chicken dinner. Silver Lay mentioned to Max that her car needed to go into the shop for service. Max said that he had some friends that owned a shop and would service her car free.

The next morning, Max drove Silver Lay's car to the shop and left it there to be fixed. He came back and told Silver Lay that the guys at the shop would fix her car for free just because they knew him well. Max said that she could pick the car up in a couple of days. Silver Lay went to Earnestine for advice about the men at the shop fixing her car free. Earnestine said, "I don't believe that, and you don't either, so stop fooling yourself about Max."

When the time came for Max to pick the car up, Silver Lay decided she wanted to go with him. They both walked to the shop. Max asked Silver Lay to pull the car out of the shop while he thanked the guys for doing such a good job on the car. Silver Lay was a little suspicious of Max and all his good gifts and the help he was getting from other people.

After they got the car from the shop, Max went out and filled the car with gas and bought back flowers, candy, and wine. He was full of surprises. They all had a good night and went to bed.

Earnestine had lived with Silver Lay and Max for two months, and she was ready to go home. She asked Max and Silver Lay to take her home on the upcoming weekend, and they agreed. When the weekend came, Earnestine packed her things to return to Mississippi. Max and Silver Lay decided that they would only be there overnight. They took an overnight bag. They left Friday morning and arrived in Mississippi at nine on Friday night. They only spent the night.

On Saturday morning they got up, cleaned up, and kissed Earnestine good-bye. They then got back into the car and headed to Chicago. After returning to Chicago, they started looking for work again.

Max's brother was a security guard. He gave Max the names of a couple security businesses that were hiring in his area. Max called the companies, and they asked him to come in for an interview. After Max got hired on the spot during one of the interviews. He was to report to work the following night. He would be working nights at a Broad-Green supermarket from seven to eleven. This meant Max would have two jobs, but he decided to let the one go that was on the west side of Chicago.

Max seemed to be very happy about his new job. This job was closer to the apartment where they lived than his other one had been. He called in and told his first supervisor that he would be leaving their firm within two weeks because he had gotten a job closer to where he lived. He again told Silver Lay that she didn't have to work and that she could stay home and take care of her daughter.

He would go to work every night and bring back roses and candy for Silver Lay. He would also bring Danielle gifts. *He is so caring,* Silver Lay thought again and again.

One morning Silver Lay's dad called her and asked why she was purchasing so many items on the Amoco credit card. She stated that she had only used it to purchase gas for the trip to Chicago. Her dad wanted to know if someone had stolen the card. She assured him that the card was in her purse and that she was going to mail it back to him. She hung the telephone up and started looking through her purse for the card, and she noticed that the card was not there. Max even asked if he could help her find the card. He looked on top of closet shelves and under clothes. He looked everywhere he could think of looking in the house. He grew tired after a while, and so did Silver Lay. Silver Lay knew the only person that she had been around was Max.

Silver Lay started thinking about all the gifts Max had been brining home every night and how he had gotten the money to pay for them. She even thought about the car and who had paid for it to be fixed. Silver Lay started thinking back to their first dinner date in Greenwood and how Max had turned his back to them while paying for the meals. She also thought about the time he purchased a train ticket to Chicago and told them to stay outside, and about all the phone calls he made without ever receiving a bill. *Oh my God!* she thought. *He is a credit card thief.*

When Max came home from work that night, he had cold cuts, chips, and a box of candy. Silver Lay knew that he must be using her dad's credit card. She finally asked Max if he had taken the Amoco credit card from her purse. He assured her that he did not have the card. Silver Lay decided to search the apartment one more time, and Max was right by her side, helping her look for her dad's credit card. They looked in closets, under clothes, under cabinet, under rugs, and under the beds. She finally realized that the card was not in the apartment.

Silver Lay's dad called the next day. He told her that the card was still being used and that bills were coming in. She suggested that he report the card as stolen. She also called Amoco and requested a copy of the signature page. She told Max that she hoped it was not his signature. He assured her that he wouldn't do a silly thing like that. Silver Lay still had her doubts. Every day, Silver Lay would meet the mailman downstairs. Max would always be by her side, watching the mailman hand the mail to Silver Lay.

The day finally came when the mailman handed Silver Lay an envelope from Amoco—one she had ordered some time before. Silver Lay walked back upstairs, carrying the Amoco envelope into their apartment. She opened it to find out that it was Max's signature. She asked him in a loud voice, "What kind of man are you, pretending that you are taking care of us while all the time my dad's credit card was taking care of us?" Max just kept trying to tell Silver Lay that was not his signature. She knew that he was lying. "How could you sleep with me and go behind my back and do such cruel things?" she asked.

It finally came time for Max to go to work. He stormed out through the door. Silver Lay and her daughter got ready for bed. Silver Lay started fixing the bed and discovered pink nail polish on the mattress. She and her daughter slept in her daughter's room. The next morning, Max woke Silver Lay up with a picture of him and a man he had caught stealing from the Broad-Greens store. Both men were smiling as though they were two of a kind. Silver Lay thought it was silly for a security guard to take a friendly picture with a criminal. She gave the picture back to him and didn't want to look at it again. She asked Max, "Why is there pink nail polish on the bed mattress." He finally told her that he had dated another woman while she was in Mississippi and that she had polished her toenails on the bed. Silver Lay walked right up to him and slapped him in the face.

He changed the conversation and started talking about how he believed he could rob the Board-Green Store where he works. He asked her if she would go to another town so he could meet her there after he robbed the store. By now he was really making her sick to her stomach. She said that was the most disgusting thing that she had ever heard.

Silver Lay and her daughter put their clothes on and left for a walk in the park. Max came running up behind them, saying he was only joking, but Silver Lay could see the seriousness in his eyes. All of a sudden, Silver Lay started feeling sick. She was only a block away from the doctor's office and didn't want to go back to the apartment with Max so soon because of all the lies he had been telling. She decided to walk on to the doctor's office. Max walked along with her. As they were walking to the doctor's office, a CTA bus drove by. They could hear young men on the bus yelling at Max, saying things like, "We are going to beat you up the next time we get close to you." Right then Silver Lay thought about what Earnestine had said about how Max was going to get her and him hurt or in trouble.

They finally made it to the doctor's office. Silver Lay signed her name in the register and took a seat. About ten minutes passed before the nurse called her name. She got up and went to the back and told the doctor her compliant. She was having pain in her breast. The doctor told the nurse to send Silver Lay to the hospital to run some tests on her. Silver Lay walked across the street to the hospital. The nurse ran some tests on her. After the tests were done, the nurse at the hospital told her to go back across the street to the doctor and wait for the nurse to call her name again.

After sitting in the waiting room for over an hour, the nurse finally called her name. She walked behind the nurse to a room in the back. The nurse told her to be seated and said that the doctor would be with her shortly. The doctor came into in the room where Silver Lay was sitting and told her that she had first-stage breast cancer.

Silver Lay said to the doctor, "Did you say breast cancer?"

There was not a smile anywhere on the doctor's face. He looked at Silver Lay and said, "Yes, breast cancer." He went on to say that he could perform outpatient surgery and remove it. He was absolutely sure that the cancer wouldn't return.

Just when Silver Lay thought things couldn't get any worse, a doctor was telling her that she has breast cancer. The doctor told her to think about surgery and get back with him. Oh yes, he also told her that the she would have to pay two hundred dollars up front for the necessary paperwork. She said okay and got up with her head hanging down and walked straight out of the doctor's office. Max came following after her, asking "What's wrong?" Silver Lay didn't say a word; she just kept her head down and started thinking about all the cruel things that he had done to her and how he had hurt her emotions.

She thought that she was too young to have breast cancer. She didn't want to go through the surgery. She thought that she hadn't come to Chicago only to find out that she had breast cancer. She had come to better herself and get a job so she could take care of her family.

They finally walked home, and Max again asked Silver Lay, "What's wrong?" Silver Lay told Max that the doctor had told her that she had breast cancer and wanted to perform surgery, but she needed two hundred dollars up front for the necessary paperwork.

Silver Lay called her sister Earnestine to tell her that the doctor had diagnosed her with breast cancer. She went on to tell Earnestine that the doctor wanted her to have outpatient surgery and that before the surgery she had to pay two hundred dollars for the necessary paperwork. Earnestine had always wanted the best for Silver Lay. She asked Silver Lay if she was sure about having surgery in Chicago, and Silver Lay said yes. The next day, Earnestine wired the money through Western Union to take care of the necessary paperwork so Silver Lay could have surgery. Max, Silver Lay, and Danielle rode the CTA bus downtown to pick the money up. While they were at the Western Union station, they saw Little Milton Campbell and asked him if he would sign his autograph on Danielle's small ball. He did and was glad to do it.

After they picked the money up, they called the doctor's office to schedule an appointment. The nurse said that she could come in the next day at eight o'clock. They went home to prepare for the surgery.

Silver Lay cooked supper early. She fixed her daughter's plate. Her daughter ate, and Silver Lay then cleaned her up to put her to bed. The next morning, they all got up bright and early and boarded the CTA bus to Robbie's house to drop Danielle off to play with Robbie's children. Robbie always welcomed them with a big hug, and she was no different this day. After they dropped Danielle off, they boarded the bus again. This time they were on their way to the clinic on Michigan Avenue.

When they arrived, Silver Lay went to the desk, signed her name, and waited in the lobby for her name to be called. The nurse eventually opened the door to the lobby. She asked Silver Lay to come to the back as Max sat in the waiting room. The doctor performed the surgery, and the nurse pushed Silver Lay to the recovery room, where she stayed for about twenty minutes. The nurse came to check on her. She checked her blood pressure and asked Silver Lay a few questions. The questions were, "can you tell me the day you was born"? "can you also tell me how old are you"? Silver Lay answered all the questions correctly.

The nurse told Silver Lay that she could go home but that she needed to stop by the front desk and pick up her prescription. Silver Lay did just that. She picked up her prescription and walked around the corner and had it filled at the drugstore. She went back to pick up the medicine after the prescription had been filled. Max and Silver Lay then rode the CTA bus to Robbie's apartment to pick up Danielle. After they picked Danielle up, they rode the CTA bus to their apartment. Silver Lay was tired and laid down to rest. After recuperating from the breast cancer, Silver Lay decided that she could no longer live with Max's lies, stealing, and cheating. She didn't know how to tell him that she no longer wanted him in her life, because by now he seemed to be obsessed with her.

She starts thinking that maybe when he left for work she would leave and catch the bus to Mississippi. Then she started pacing the floor, thinking that if he caught her he might hurt her for trying to leave him. *Oh my God!* she thought.

She decided to just tell him that she would be taking a trip to Mississippi to visit with her friends and relatives. Silver Lay finally made up her mind and went to the living room and told Max that she thought it was time for her to take a trip to Mississippi. He agreed that she could go to Mississippi as long as she was back in two weeks. She agreed with him and asked him to take her and Danielle to the bus station. Max thought that Silver Lay was going to return to Chicago, but she had no intention of returning. She just wanted to get away without any kind of confrontation.

CHAPTER 8

Strings of Harassment

After Silver Lay arrived in Mississippi, Max started calling and asking her when she would be coming back to Chicago. She said, "Never, never, never again." She told him that she could not live with him anymore. In a relaxed voice, she said, "I am home to stay." She recounted all the things that he had done to destroy their relationship. She told him about her dad's Amoco credit card and how Max had faked helping her look for the card while he had it all the time. He had really made her look very stupid. She told him that he had cheated on her with the lady down the hall from where they lived. "How could you?" she asked. "How could you put me and my daughter in danger? She said that you would go out at night and do crazy things like arrest people and tell them that you were not going to turn them over to the police. And why? You were putting our lives in danger. Every time those people see us, they start throwing things off the CTA bus at us and using profanity. I believe in my heart that you are a credit card thief."

Silver Lay went on to refresh his mind about their lunch in Greenwood, his engagement ring, their bus ticket, her car repair, and the candy, wine, and gifts he bought for her and her daughter. "I don't want to live off other people's incomes," she said, and she hung up on him.

Max kept calling, sometimes three times a day. After Max found out that Silver Lay was serious about not coming back to him, he decided to call and threaten her by saying such things as, "If I can't have you, nobody will." He told her that he was coming to Mississippi to hurt her and whatever man friend she had. He kept calling every day for the next fourteen days. He said the same things every day.

Silver Lay decided to get her telephone number changed. She thought that she would never hear from him again. Max started calling people that he knew she associated with. He called a lady that worked at a grocery store and asked her to tell Silver Lay to go back to him or that he would have no other choice but to come to Mississippi and hurt her. He called another lady in the town where Silver Lay lived. He asked her to encourage Silver Lay to go back to Chicago to be with him.

The ladies he called informed Silver Lay of what Max had said. At this point in time, Silver Lay didn't want to hear anything about Max. She asked the young ladies to please not tell her anything that Max said anymore.

Max wanted Silver Lay's new telephone number. He called her sister Sugar. Sugar always liked Max and thought he was absolutely harmless. She invited him to come down for Christmas and talk with Silver Lay himself. He came down for Christmas and stayed with Sugar for the holiday. Silver Lay didn't know that Max was staying with Sugar, though. She didn't even know that he was coming down at all. Sugar kept it a secret from Silver Lay and Earnestine.

On Christmas Eve Danielle's dad called to ask Silver Lay if he could take Danielle to breakfast with him and his boys. She said yes. The telephone rang again, and it was Sugar wanting to know if she could come to Silver Lay's house for a surprise visit. Silver Lay said yes because she thought Sugar had gifts that she wanted to give her. Silver Lay told Earnestine that Danielle's dad was coming to take Danielle to breakfast and to let him know that they would be at Sugar's house.

They walked up the street to Sugar's house, and as they entered the front door, Danielle's dad pulled up. He got out of his truck and came in to pick his daughter up for breakfast. Minutes later, Max walked in the house as if it were a setup. He attacked Danielle's dad, hitting him in the face and giving him a black eye. "Oh no!" Silver Lay said with a look of surprise on her face. She grabbed Max by the shirt, trying to stop him from hitting Danielle's dad. Sugar came into the living room and called Max's name. He finally stopped fighting. When it was over, Danielle's dad got into the truck and drove away without taking Danielle to breakfast. Silver Lay and her daughter walked back down the street toward home. Silver Lay was deeply hurt. She and Danielle went inside, and she locked the door.

The next day was Christmas, and Max went to Earnestine's house to give Danielle some presents that he had brought from Chicago. He knocked on the door, and Silver Lay asked her sister to please not open the door. She was a nervous wreck and was very afraid of him. Earnestine assured Silver Lay that she would not let him in the house. She answered the door and told him that Silver Lay didn't want to see him anymore. He walked away, carrying the gifts back to Sugar's house. Silver Lay's knees were shaking.

Silver Lay was a nervous wreck. She had to go lie down. She was in fear for her life. She thought for sure that Max would try to hurt her. When Max returned to Sugar's house, he told her that Silver Lay refused to see him. Sugar told Max that she would take the gifts to Silver Lay. She got the gifts from Max and walked to Earnestine's house. She knocked on the door and Earnestine said, "Come in." Sugar wished them all a Merry Christmas and told Earnestine that she had some gifts for Silver Lay and Danielle that Max had bought. Earnestine said that Max had just left with the gifts and Silver Lay didn't want to see him.

Sugar went into the room where Silver Lay was lying and tried to encourage her to except the gifts. She refused to accept the gifts and told Sugar that she didn't want to see Max or anything that he had. Sugar told Silver Lay that she didn't think it was such a big deal. She gathered the gifts and walked back up the street to her house. Silver Lay was still lying in bed. Her strength seemed to be leaving fast. She was getting tired of Max trying to force himself into her life.

Danielle went into the room where her mom was lying. She asked her for some candy. They didn't have any candy at home, so Silver Lay decided to drive her to the store to get some candy. They had to go past Danielle's dad's house to get to the store. On their way to the store, the passenger car door came open and

Danielle leaned over headfirst outside the car. One of her little hands touched the ground. Silver Lay pulled her up very fast. She was unharmed. She told her mom that she had lost some of her money. Her mother replied, "Don't you worry about that. I will give you some more money. I am just so glad that you didn't get hurt." She hugged her and kissed her on the forehead. When they arrived at the store, Danielle bought candy and a pop. She was so happy.

Silver Lay decided that she would stop by Danielle's dad's house to apologize for Max's actions. She knocked at the door, and he said, "Come right in." She entered the door and tried to explain Max's actions. She apologized for the way he had reacted toward him. Danielle's dad was very easygoing. He immediately said he accepted her apology.

Danielle's dad said that he would forgive that man for her. She and Danielle got back in the car and started driving home. When they drove up to a stop sign, all of a sudden Max jumped out from some bushes. He asked her to stop the car. She rolled the car windows up and locked the doors. Max jumped on the trunk of the car with his arms and legs stretched wide, as though he were in control of the car. She put the car in reverse and then back in drive again, slamming down on the brakes, wishing he would fall off the car. Max was still holding on. She did it again, and that time it seemed to her that he jumped to the side of the car.

Silver Lay called her sister Earnestine and told her about what had happened. She asked her sister to wait at the front door because she was on her way home. Silver Lay drove to house and found her sister waiting by the door. She parked the car in the driveway and grabbed Danielle by the hand and ran inside. She sat down and looked at Earnestine and said that she was tired of Max stalking her.

She didn't know where Max may be. She really hated that her sister had invited him to come down for the holiday. She was so afraid that if he caught her, he was going to hurt her. She said Sugar just didn't know the seriousness of the situation between her and Max. She hadn't told Sugar because Sugar thought Max was harmless. She really didn't want to talk about it anyway because it hurt so badly. All she wanted him to do was stay away from her, but he insisted that either he would be around her or nobody would.

The pressure was great. Silver Lay had gotten to the point where all she wanted to do was stay in bed. It seemed that she could not think straight. The only thing she was thinking about was Max hurting her and how she could prevent it.

The holidays ended and Max finally went back home to Chicago. She thought everything was finally over. "He can't call me anymore," she said to herself. But the day after he got back to Chicago, Max was back on the telephone, threatening her. Once again he was telling her that he was going to hurt her.

One day she answered the telephone and asked him how he had gotten her telephone number. He replied, "I have a way of getting what I want." Silver Lay hung the telephone up in fear of being hurt by Max. She knew that Sugar had given Max her telephone number. He called every day and night, telling her that he was going to kill her. Silver Lay had only to answer the telephone and he would scream through it, saying the same thing every day: "I am going to hurt you."

Silver Lay stopped answering the telephone and started staying in bed most of the time, sometimes all day. She stayed in bed even when she wasn't sleeping, and some days she wouldn't eat. She felt as though she was losing touch with reality. She was drifting away in her own self-pity.

One day Penny Line came over and asked her to drive her to the store. She really didn't want to get out of bed, but she didn't want to say no to Penny Line. She pulled herself from bed, got dressed quickly, and hurriedly drove Penny Line to the store. It seemed as though Silver Lay always did things in a hurry now. When they arrived at the store, Silver Lay decided that she was going to get out of the car.

CHAPTER 9

Being Depressed

Silver Lay got out of the car and went inside the store. She felt as though she was going to pass out on the floor. She wanted to turn around and get back in the car and get back to the house as fast as she could so she could get back to bed. It seemed as though the bed was her comfort zone now. She was going out of her mind in fear of Max. She felt as though the whole world was on top of her and she couldn't find her way out.

Silver Lay felt she couldn't be around people. She was afraid to go to stores because her heart would start racing and her mind would tell her to do things like pass out on the store floor or start running. She knew those were the wrong things to do, so she would stay home and stay in bed until she felt better.

Earnestine grew concerned about the way Silver Lay was lying in bed, drifting away from society. She called Sugar over to check on Silver Lay. Sugar came over and said to Silver Lay, "You need to stop being so upset about Max because he doesn't mean any harm. He just loves you and wants to be with you." Sugar left and walked back up the street to her house.

Silver Lay decided she would get another private number. She called the telephone company, and the company changed the number as they were speaking. Silver Lay told Earnestine that she was not going to give the number to anyone, and Earnestine agreed that she should not. Silver Lay still believed that Sugar gave Max her first private number because Sugar wanted her to get back with him and because Sugar thought Max was harmless. She knew that he was melting her down mentally.

After Silver Lay got the private number, she went back to bed and drifted away under the covers. Earnestine was still concerned about her sister and called Woodrow to come and check on her. Woodrow was getting ready for bed but told Earnestine that he would be there soon. He got back in his clothes and went outside and got in his truck and drove to Earnestine's house to see Silver Lay. He found her in bed, just as Earnestine had said. Her face was underneath the covers. Woodrow pulled the covers from her face. He asked what the problem was. She said, "I am not feeling well." Drifting off in her own self-pity, she said to Woodrow, "Please don't leave me alone, because I might need you to take me to the hospital."

He replied, "When you need me, I'll be around, but you need to get in control of your emotions, because even a crazy person doesn't think he is crazy. Now, if a crazy person thinks he has sense, how much more are you supposed to know that you have sense?"

Silver Lay looked straight into her brother's eyes and didn't say a word; she was just thinking he was right. He said, "Call me if you need me." She said she would, and he left for home.

After her brother left for home, Silver Lay thought about how Woodrow knew the seriousness of her problem. He had just gone through a nasty divorce. He knew that she was suffering mentally. He wanted her to put her thoughts back in the right perspective. It seem to her as though her mind was racing with unpleasant thoughts. She wanted to turn the thoughts off. She took Woodrow's advice because she believed in him. Woodrow had gone through some serious problems in his life.

She went and bought a tape of sounds of crashing waves to listen to as she tried to put her thoughts back in the right perspective. When her mind tried to produce one negative thought, she would produce two positive thoughts. She would listen to the tape every night and sometimes in the daytime. Silver Lay was really training her mind to think positive thoughts again. It was a slow process, and she wanted a quick fix.

Sugar and her friend had joined an uptown church named Church of Christ. Earnestine asked Sugar to invite Silver Lay to some of the services to get her out of the bed. Sugar told Earnestine that Silver Lay was just being mean to Max and wanted him to chase after her, although she did ask Silver Lay if she would like to come to the service with them. She agreed to go to the service because she had always heard during her mother's time on earth that God can do all things and will never fail you.

She knew that she wanted her positive thoughts to override her negative thoughts. They went to several of the services and got baptized at the Church of Christ. Silver Lay had been taught that in order to be saved, people must be baptized in the name of the Father, the Son, and the Holy Ghost. She had also heard that if someone chokes on the water, that meant the person hadn't received the Holy Ghost.

When Silver Lay went under the water during her baptism, she choked. Sugar said that she hadn't received the Holy Ghost and would need to be baptized again. Silver Lay was very upset when Sugar told her that she would need to be baptized again. The pastor didn't tell her anything about needing to be baptized again. When you get baptized at a church, that means you have become an official member of that church because you have joined through water—whether you choke or not. They continued to meet for services every Sunday.

Silver Lay would walk to Sugar's house with the Bible in her hand to catch a ride to church. She would go and sit on the pew but didn't get anything out of the services because she didn't have an open mind. Her mind was still fighting negative thoughts. She still thought Max was coming to hurt her.

She left church one week and went back to lying in bed again. Silver Lay told Earnestine that she would get help for herself. The next day, Silver Lay called a mental health facility in a nearby town to make an appointment to see a therapist. The therapist set up an appointment for the next day.

The next day, Silver Lay got ready to go see the therapist. She was a little afraid to go alone, so she invited Earnestine to go with her. Earnestine agreed to go; she even told Silver Lay that she would pretend she was the one that needed to see the therapist if someone walked in that knew Silver Lay. Silver Lay smiled at that. They took a seat in the waiting area, and Silver Lay's name was soon called to register to see a therapist. The receptionist asked

Silver Lay if Earnestine was part of her problem. Silver Lay said, "I really don't think so; why do you ask?"

The receptionist said, "The person that sticks right by your side is usually the one that's at fault."

Silver Lay started thinking about this, and she realized that Earnestine had agreed with all the negative thoughts that had been coming into her head. She had told Earnestine that she believed Max was serious about hurting her, and Earnestine had agreed. In fact, Earnestine agreed with every negative thought that Silver Lay had had. That was not helping Silver Lay build positive thoughts. Silver Lay didn't think Earnestine was trying to harm her in any way; she just thought that Earnestine loved her and didn't know how to help her out of the situation that she was in.

Silver Lay looked at Earnestine and looked at the receptionist and said that she didn't believe Earnestine was her problem. She then returned to her seat in the waiting room. A male therapist called her to the back. The man greeted her with a smile and told her that he wanted to get acquainted with her. He told her his name, and she introduced herself.

He wanted to know what had brought her there, and she told him that Max was the reason she was there. He wanted to know who Max was. She told him that he was her former companion that she had lived with in Chicago. She said she had left him because he was a liar, a cheater, and a thief. She explained that he had made her feel weak and afraid of him by constantly telling her that he was going to come to Mississippi and hurt her, and that she believed it. The therapist wrote her information down and told her that during her next visit he would pretend to be

Max; he wanted her to tell Max everything that was on her mind concerning him. He opened his office door and let her out. Silver Lay went to the front desk and made an appointment for the next month. Silver Lay and Earnestine then left for home.

Silver Lay said that she thought the therapist was going to help her with her negative thoughts. Earnestine said maybe he would on the next visit.

When they arrived home, Silver Lay went right back to bed; that was her comfort zone. She was still very weak in the mind. She still thought that Max was coming to hurt her. The next day, her brother came over. He asked her if she would go to town and pay some bills for him. She agreed to go pay his bills. She didn't want to, but she didn't know how to tell him that she was not ready to face society. She believed Woodrow was trying to keep her out of bed.

She dragged herself from the bed and got dressed. She got into her car and went to town to pay Woodrow's bills. She drove to the electric company and had to force herself to get out of the car. She went through the door and wanted to turn and run back out. She nervously stayed in line until it was time for her to pay the bill. She paid the bill and nervously walked back to her car. That was one of the hardest things she had ever done.

She went to the gas company to pay Woodrow's gas bill. She nervously forced herself from the car and went inside to pay the gas bill. She stayed in line with her eyes straight in front of her, not looking at anyone but the teller. She paid the money to the teller and hurriedly exited through the door. She rushed to her car and took a deep breath, and then she drove off to her house. Silver Lay felt as though she couldn't be successful in society and couldn't be around people or have conversations with people. She thought that she might pass out.

The next day, Silver Lay got dressed to see the therapist for the second time, and Earnestine went along. Silver Lay arrived at her appointed time. She signed in and took a seat. The therapist came to the waiting room and called her name. She got up to go to his office, and he said, "Welcome, come on in and have a seat," with a big smile. He asked her to pretend that he was Max and let all her hurt feelings out toward him. She just smiled and started talking about how the thought of him made her feel weak and nervous.

The therapist asked her, "When you talk about him, how does it make you feel?"

"Nervous," she said. She couldn't pretend that the therapist was Max because she couldn't stand to say Max's name. The therapist said the more she practiced saying Max's name, the better she would feel. Silver Lay didn't agree with the therapist, because it seemed to her that if he or anyone else called Max's name around her, she would lose all capacity for thought for a moment. He suggested that they talk more about Max on the next visit. He opened the door to let her out and thanked her for coming in.

Silver Lay didn't schedule an appointment for the next month. She and Earnestine left for home. On the way home, Silver Lay told Earnestine that she could talk to her and get the same result. She didn't feel as though the therapy was helping her with her mental problem. She still felt very weak and afraid of Max. Her thoughts about herself were still negative. The therapist asks who was coming with her, and she said, "My sister."

The therapist said, "Your sister feels responsible for some of the things that you are going through."

CHAPTER 10

Breaking Point

Silver Lay started thinking that her sister was a nice woman who was not responsible for any of her actions. Earnestine just didn't know what to tell her to keep her from being afraid of Max. Silver Lay didn't know what to do, because the therapy sessions were not working for her. Her sisters and brother gave her advice, and she joined an uptown church and visited a therapist, but nothing seemed to work. She knew that she couldn't keep trying to watch over her own life. She couldn't continue staying awake at night. She knew that this problem was bigger than she was. She was at her breaking point. She rolled out of her bed, fell to her knees, and crawled to her bedroom window, looking toward the blue sky while crying, "Lord, Lord, Lord, please help me."

A thought came to her mind. *It seems that you have tried everything else; now it is time to get serious with God and try him.* She read the following passage in the Bible:

But thou, when thou prayest, enter into thy closet, and when thou hast shut thy door, pray to thy Father which is in secret; and thy Father which seeth in secret shall reward thee openly. But when ye pray, use not vain repetitions as the heathen do; for they think that they shall reward thee openly. But when ye pray, use not vain repetitions as the heathen do: for they think that they shall be heard for their much speaking. Be not ye therefore like unto them: for your Father knoweth what things ye have need of, before ye ask him. After this manner therefore pray ye:

Our Father which are in heaven, Hallowed be thy name. Thy Kingdom come. Thy will be done in earth, as it is in heaven. Give us this day our daily bread. And forgive us our debts, as we forgive our debtors. And lead us not into temptation, but deliver us from evil: For thine is the kingdom, and the power, and the glory, forever. Amen. (Matthew 6:6–13 KJV)

After reading this prayer in the King James Version, she decided to go in her closet and pray a serious prayer to the Lord. She prayed, "Father—not just my Father, but everyone's Father—I am not selfish, Father, just in need. I believe you are in heaven. I believe you died for our sins. Holy is your name. I believe that one day your kingdom will come to earth and that whatever has been recorded on earth will be recorded in heaven." It seemed as though something was speaking for her. She kept speaking, saying, "Father, feed me thy holy word that I may learn not to hold anything in my heart against anyone. Teach me to love everyone. Father, keep me away from the pathway of evil. Father, please help me to think right. Father, I am so tired of staying awake at night in fear of Max coming to hurt me. I realize that my life belongs to you. I know that you gave me life and you can take my life. My life I put in your hands. I will leave everything up to you." With that, she fell asleep inside of the closet.

Her brother came to the house to eat dinner before he went to work. He went to Silver Lay's room to see how she was doing, and he found that she was not in bed. He walked over to the closet and saw her lying in a curled-up position. He closed the door and went back to the kitchen to inform Earnestine that she was in the closet.

Woodrow, Earnestine, and Danielle sat down to eat dinner. When Woodrow finished, he kiss Danielle on the forehead and left for work. Silver Lay finally got out of the closet and went to eat dinner. By this time she was feeling much better. She read a story to Danielle and went back to bed.

Silver Lay now knew what made her feel better. She continued to go into the closet every morning; there she would close the door and start praying the prayer from Matthew 6:6–13. She remembered what she had read in the Bible: "... thy Father which is in secret; and thy Father which seeth in secret shall reward thee openly."

She knew that she was in no position to keep trying to hold her life in her own hands. She had to let it all go and let God take over. At the same time, her mind was being trained with responsible thoughts because God is responsible and does just what he says he will do. Silver Lay knew that if she kept her mind on God and all the responsible things that he had done, then she would also learn not to fear, because God is not of fear, and once again she would have a responsible mind.

Every day, Silver Lay felt a little better than the day before. It seemed as though the weight of the world was lifting off her body. One day she asked Earnestine if she wanted to walk over to Woodrow's house with her. Silver Lay wanted to walk to see if she could face people again. Earnestine agreed to walk over to Woodrow's house with Silver Lay. She noticed Silver Lay was walking fast and staring straight ahead. When they got to Woodrow's house, Silver Lay took a deep breath, as though that was one of the hardest things that she had ever done.

They rang the doorbell, and Woodrow asked them to come in. They insisted that he come outside and sit with them. He agreed and started talking about Modern Line; he loved that place. It was a factory where he had worked for years. As he often did, he told them about his little black book and all the codes that he had in the book to help him run the dials in the press room. He said the guys on the shifts wouldn't tell him how to set the dials correctly, so he had to pay attention and write down everything that he learned from the boss. He kept the information in a black book in his lunch box, which he kept locked up in the locker room.

Whenever he needed to know something about setting a dial, he would run to the locker room, read the little black book, and run back to the press room and fix it. After he finished his story, Silver Lay and Earnestine told Woodrow that they had to go home and that it had been nice talking to him. He said, "I hate to see you go. Do you want something to drink?"

They declined the drink, thanked him, and walked back home. Silver Lay didn't feel as if she were going to pass out or start running. After that, Silver Lay began to feel good about herself and God. The next morning, she went back into her closet, closed the door, and repeated the Our Father prayer:

> Our Father which are in Heaven, Hallow be thy name. Thy kingdom come. Thy will be done in earth, as it is in heaven. Give us this day our daily bread. And forgive us this day our daily bread. And forgive us our debts, as we forgive our debtors. And lead us not into temptation, but deliver us from evil: For thine is the Kingdom, and the power, and the glory, forever. Amen. (Matthew 6:9–13 KJV)

CHAPTER 11

Regaining Her Life through Christ

Silver Lay started noticing that the more she prayed, the better she felt. She seemed to be more responsible for herself. She started thinking that her issues were not about Max but about God. With her mind on God and all of his goodness, she started feeling like a part of society again. She could talk with people again, walk with people again. She could even go to the grocery store without feeling as if she were going to pass out or just start running. Silver Lay started sitting outside again. Penny Line would come over, and they would engage in conversation about Silver Lay's daughter again. Everything was getting back to normal.

Earnestine called Silver Lay one day and asked her to go to the store for her. This time Earnestine was having barbecue, and she needed some barbecue sauce. Penny Line went to the store with her. Silver Lay noticed that when she entered the store, she didn't feel like passing out or running without a cause. Silver Lay and

Penny Line both got their shopping carts and shopped for their items. They met back at the checkout counter.

Silver Lay even met some people that she knew in the store. She spoke to them, and they spoke back. She talked to them about how hot the weather was. She ended the conversation when Penny Line checked out at the counter. She said that she would see them later. She then went to the checkout counter herself and checked out. She and Penny Line got back into the car and went home. When they arrived at home, she gave Earnestine the barbecue sauce. Earnest marinated the meat for the next day.

Silver Lay started visiting an uptown church in the town where she lived. She attended regular services there. She even went to Sunday school. She was still hearing good things about the Lord. The Word was replacing her negative thoughts with positive thoughts. She started visiting more churches in different towns. Every church that she visited taught her about the goodness of the Lord.

Do you remember how Silver Lay always wanted a job? Well, about eighteen miles away from where she lived, she was called in for an interview for a teaching position. She went in for the interview, and the superintendent interviewed her and asked the principal to show her around the schools.

She felt very comfortable about getting the position as an elementary teacher. The principal asked her which school she thought she would be comfortable at. She told him the elementary school would be best. Without any hesitation, they went straight to the elementary school. He introduced her to the principal and some of the resource teacher classes. In one of the resource teacher rooms, she saw a little girl jump through a window and start running. The window was almost at the ground level. Some of the teachers and the janitors ran behind her. The finally caught the little girl and brought her back to the school.

Right then and there Silver Lay decided that she wouldn't be comfortable at the elementary school. She told the principal that she was ready to observe the high school. He drove her there. They went into the building and walked down the hall to a resource class. The students were not ready for a new teacher at that point. They wanted to keep their substitute teacher.

Silver Lay liked the high school because the students were more advanced than the elementary students. She knew that she could work diligently with these students without having to run behind them. The principal took her back to the superintendent's office and dropped her off. She walked in, and the superintendent asked her which school she would prefer to work at. She told him she preferred the high school.

The superintendent looked at her with a smile and asked, "Why do you have the credentials but are not employed in your profession?" Silver Lay just smiled back because she knew that she had gone to Chicago looking for work that paid more than working in her profession. Silver Lay thought then that she must have been looking in all the wrong places in Chicago.

From the time she was a small child, she had always had a passion for children. She thought, *Now here I am, finally getting the position that I want, only eighteen miles away from home.*

The superintendent asked her, "What day would you like to start working, because you have the job."

She replied, "Monday." She was so excited. She went back home to let Earnestine know that she had gotten the job that she had always wanted.

Silver Lay went into her closet, shut the door, and started praying: "Our Father which art in heaven, Hallowed be thy name. Thy kingdom come. Thy will be done in earth, as it is in heaven. Give us this day our daily bread. And forgive us our debts, as we forgive our debtors. And lead us not into temptation, but deliver us from evil: For thine is the kingdom, and the power, and the glory, for ever. Amen."

She started praising God, thanking him for all that he had done for her. Her sister Earnestine had always told her that if she thanked God for the small things, he would bless her with larger things.

Since the most recent time Silver Lay got her phone number changed, Max hadn't gotten it. Silver Lay believed that he couldn't get the telephone number, because Sugar had found out the seriousness of Silver Lay's case. She really didn't want to see her sister's health deteriorate.

Silver Lay hadn't heard from Max or any of his associates for about two months. Her life was really mending back together well. She decided to join an uptown church. She went to church there every Sunday, and she even went to Sunday school. The pastor asked her one day, "Would you like to be baptized?" She said yes. Then he asked her if she believed in the Scripture John 3:16, and she said yes again.

He asked her to read it, and she did: "For God so loved the world, that he gave his only begotten son, that whosoever believeth in him should not perish, but have everlasting life."

After service one Friday night, everyone that wanted to be baptized was allowed to take part in the baptism ceremony. Silver Lay started thinking about the time when she was baptized at the Church of Christ. She hadn't held her breath, and although the pastor had her nose covered with a towel, she choked when the pastor lowered her backward underneath the water. Sugar told her that she hadn't received the Holy Ghost because of that.

Now she was ready to be baptized again. She marched in the line with her head high in the air. She was thinking to herself that nothing could stop her from receiving the Holy Ghost this time. She finally marched to the top of the stairs and looked down into the water, saying to herself that she was ready for this. The pastor held his hand out to help her step down into the water.

She walked very slowly down the steps, turned, and faced the members of the congregation. Her pastor placed a towel over her nose. He bent her backward under the water and brought her up quickly. She was so proud of herself; she had held her breath under the water and hadn't choked this time. When the pastor helped her out of the water, she felt very relaxed.

Earnestine was there to congratulate Silver Lay on her Baptism. She gave her a big hug as all the members of the church marched around and gave all the people who had been baptized a hug. Silver Lay felt in her heart that God had forgiven her for all of her sins and would never remember them again.

It seemed as though every day was getting better and better for Silver Lay now that Max was out of her life. She was not hearing anything from him anymore. She had started teaching school too. All the puzzle pieces of her life that had been missing seem to be falling back into place. She was very happy, and she was leading a normal life now. She would go to work every day and to church on Sunday. Sometimes the church held services during the week as well. Silver Lay was enjoying her life once again.

One day, Silver Lay's dad's aunt asked Silver Lay's dad to come to Chicago for the weekend to help her with some family business. He asked Silver Lay and Sugar if they would like to come alone for the ride. They said no because they didn't have any money. He insisted that they go and said he would take care of the expenses. It was summer and they didn't have anything else to do, so Silver Lay and Sugar decided that they would go to Chicago with their dad. He asked them to be ready the next morning at eight o'clock. They packed their bags Thursday night and got a good night's rest. They were to travel in their dad's car. Riding all the way to Chicago in a car is not a comfortable trip; Silver Lay had traveled to and from Chicago many times, and she knew how uncomfortable the ride could be, but she thought that she was up to the trip.

The next morning, their dad drove to Silver Lay's house, where Sugar and Silver Lay were waiting to be picked up. They got in the car, and he left for Chicago. They rode all day. They finally arrived in Chicago at his aunt house around eight o'clock that night. She came out and greeted them with a hug and asked them to come in.

They all went in and sat on the sofa. Their dad and his aunt started a conversation about the south and how they liked being in the north. Their dad's aunt said that she had gotten tired of picking cotton and moved to the north. Life was much better in Chicago for her. She finally said, "That is enough talking about the north and south. It is getting late. Now go get your luggage from the car, and I will show you where you will be sleeping. I know you are tired from the long ride."

They all went and got their luggage and returned to the living room where their aunt was waiting. She took their dad to a downstairs bedroom, and Sugar and Silver Lay went to an upstairs bedroom. They were really tired, so they took their bath and went to bed. Their dad's aunt was going to have a barbecue for them Saturday.

The next morning, they got dressed and came downstairs. They said good morning to everyone. They noticed their dad's aunt was preparing the meat for the barbecue. They went outside and sat on the carport.

As they were sitting there, Max came from around the north side of the carport. He said, "Good morning, ladies."

Sugar said, "Good morning to you too."

Silver Lay didn't say a word. She sat there staring at Max as if he were a ghost. She started to think that this had to be another setup, but she didn't know who could have done such a thing. She grew nervous and began shaking in her seat with her hands clenched together. She didn't know who had called Max to the house. Her dad's aunt came out through the door with her cleaning kit. Max said, "Good morning. Are you going to barbecue?"

She said, "Yes, and you are more than welcome to come. A friend of these girls is a friend of mine." She then walked around the side of the house and started cleaning the barbecue grill.

Max asked Silver Lay if she wanted to go ride the CTA bus so they could talk. She replied, "I don't want you; there is nothing to talk about. Stay away from me." She got up and ran into the house and went up to the upstairs bedroom. She got in the bed and covered her head. Max had upset her, and Sugar knew it.

Sugar left Max outside and went upstairs to the room Silver Lay was in. She asked Silver Lay why she was in bed. Silver Lay said that she didn't want to see Max or hear anything from him. Sugar asked her to get out of the bed and not let Max upset her. Silver Lay got out of the bed. Sugar looked out the bedroom window and saw Max along the side of the house with their dad and their dad's aunt. They seemed to be engaged in a conversation. Sugar raised the window to hear what they were talking about. Max told their dad's aunt that he really wanted Silver Lay back in his life. Her dad's aunt asks him to stay for the barbecue so he might get a chance to talk with her. Max sat outside for hours.

Finally it came time to eat. Their aunt called them for dinner. Silver Lay refused to come down and eat. Sugar got some food for herself and Silver Lay and started up the stairway to take the food to the room where they would be sleeping. She looked behind her and noticed that Max was following her. She turned quickly and asked him not to come up the stairs behind her because Silver Lay didn't want to see him anymore.

He slowly turned around and walked back down the staircase and out of the house. Sugar and Silver Lay ate in the room. After they finished, Sugar took their empty plates downstairs. She didn't see Max anywhere. She went back upstairs to let Silver Lay know that Max was gone. Silver Lay told Sugar that she would not feel comfortable until she got back to her hometown. Silver Lay and Sugar packed their luggage and went to bed. They would be leaving for home the next day.

They got up early the next morning and started packing their luggage. After packing, they put their bags in the car, but their dad was not ready to go. Sugar and Silver Lay insisted they leave that morning. His aunt told him to go ahead and take them home. He put his luggage in the car, and they all said good-bye to their aunt. Their dad wanted to know why they were in such a hurry to get home. Silver Lay and Sugar didn't say a word. Silver Lay was thinking that she didn't want to see Max again. Their dad started driving, but he would only go up to around fifty miles an hour. It seemed to be the longest ride they had ever taken. Perhaps it was a way of punishing them for wanting to leave that morning instead of in the evening.

When they got to a small town in Mississippi called Ruleville, Their dad pulled into a gas station. Sugar saw one of her friends getting gas and asked him to take her and Silver Lay home. "Get in," he said. They got their luggage from their dad's car and put it in Sugar's friend's car. He drove them home. They thanked him, and he drove off. Silver Lay was glad to be back at home with her small family. She went into her prayer closet and started praying. She knew that God would be with her in the closet, outside of the closet, in Chicago, or in Indianola. She started praying: "Our Father which art in heaven, Hallowed be thy name. Thy kingdom come. Thy will be done in earth, as it is in heaven. Give us this day our daily bread. And forgive us our debts, as we forgive our debtors. And lead us not into temptation, but deliver us from evil: For thine is the kingdom. And the power, and the glory, for ever. Amen."

She felt much better after her prayer. She got a good night's sleep and went to work the next day. She continued to attended church on Sundays and sometimes through the week.

As time went by Silver Lay began to feel more responsible for herself once again. Max didn't have her new telephone number, and she was not hearing anything from him or the people that he knew in Indianola anymore.

One day her pastor asked her if she would like to be a Sunday school teacher. She accepted the position and taught small children about the goodness of Jesus and how they could be saved. She continued teaching in the public school in Mississippi and worked with many small children.

Silver Lay is now an evangelist, and her job is helping people. She has mastered some of the things that she wanted to master in life. She learned from her experience and began to make better choices in life. She received a closer walk with the Lord.

Silver Lay realized that sometimes you really don't have to go far to accomplish your dreams. She started praying because prayer is the key to the kingdom, and because God taught his disciples and many others how to pray. Prayer should be written upon your heart and never forgotten. Pray this prayer at all times—especially times of need:

"Our Father which art in heaven,
Hallow be thy name.
Thy kingdom come.
Thy will be done in earth,
as it is in heaven.
Give us this day our daily bread.
And forgive us our debts,
As we forgive our debtors.
And lead us not into temptation,
But deliver us from evil:
For thin is the kingdom.
And the power,
And the glory,
For ever. Amen."